D1621211

C153715516

# IN THE
# FACE
## OF THE
# ENEMY

To those men of 'L' Sub, 30/46 Battery, 10th Field Regiment RA, and to those in 'D' Troop, 'H' Battery, 13th (HAC) Regiment RHA, with whom I had the honour of serving.

# IN THE FACE OF THE ENEMY

A Battery Sergeant Major in Action
in the Second World War

ERNEST POWDRILL MC

Pen & Sword
**MILITARY**

First published in Great Britain in 2008 by
Pen & Sword Military
an imprint of
Pen & Sword Books Ltd
47 Church Street
Barnsley
South Yorkshire
S70 2AS

ISBN: 978 1 84415 850 8

The right of this work
has e

A CIP catalogu ritish Library

All rights reserv or transmitted
in any forn including
photocopying, re etrieval system,
witl ɪg.

Printed and bound in England by MPG Biddles Ltd

*Pen & Sword Books Ltd incorporates the imprints of:*
Pen & Sword Aviation, Pen & Sword Maritime, Pen & Sword Military,
Wharncliffe Local History, Pen & Sword Select,
Pen & Sword Military Classics, Leo Cooper, Remember When,
Seaforth Publishing and Frontline Publishing.

*For a complete list of Pen & Sword titles please contact:*
Pen & Sword Books Limited
47 Church Street, Barnsley, South Yorkshire, S70 2AS, England
E-mail: enquiries@pen-and-sword.co.uk
Website: www.pen-and-sword.co.uk

# Contents

# List of Maps

# Introduction

**Background**

In setting down the events and activities in which I was engaged in the Second World War, I do so not with the intent of attracting notoriety, nor of self-seeking in any way, but to exorcize from my mind the atmosphere of war as I saw it. To take part in a battle, where the aim is to take ground by killing or disabling the enemy, is horrible by any standards, and is only redeemed by knowing that what one does is in the interests of one's country, and ultimately one's self.

To that end, I have confined myself to the two operations in which I took part – the British Expeditionary Force in May 1940 and the European Campaign in 1944. I was not in contact with enemy in between those two operations, and that period only receives attention when it bears directly on the pursuit of those objectives. My aim, therefore, is to show by narration the day-to-day events in battle as I experienced them. I am not a professional historian, although I have read widely many of the relevant books on the subject. That process has enabled me to put some of the narrative into the overall context of the war.

Part I, dealing with the 1940 campaign, relies entirely on memory. I have no notes of that period as the keeping of diaries was strictly forbidden,[1] and the literature on the subject is surprisingly rare. Nevertheless, I can remember sufficient to outline events as they occurred more or less on a daily basis.

We had gone to war, of course, with a sense of high idealism in preventing the realization of Adolph Hitler's territorial ambitions, even though the attacks on the Low Countries and France were only a prelude, as I later knew, to his intentions in the East, namely, Russia. Hitler's incremental expeditions in the Saar, Sudetenland, Austria, Czechoslovakia and Poland, were matters uncongenial to the rest of the civilized world, and they came to a head in September 1939 when Britain declared war on Germany. France's declaration came some hours later.

I joined the Territorial Army in 1935 and transferred to the Regular

---

1 It is surprising how many senior and junior officers managed to keep detailed diaries, whilst we, at the other end of the scale, were forbidden to do so. The reason was, no doubt, that at the 'sharp end' we were more likely to be captured by the enemy, and a diary might give away matters of interest to enemy Intelligence.

Army in 1938. By August 1939 I had reached the rank of full gun sergeant in 30/46 Battery of the 10th Field Regiment, Royal Artillery, the same month that we mobilized for war. Mobilization came as no surprise – we had been expecting it for weeks, if not months. Store sheds, which had been under permanent lock and key, were opened. Reservists were recalled to the colours, and the Regiment, comprised of two batteries, reformed itself into twenty-four gun subsections, each of six men, headed by a full gun sergeant. My gun was numbered 'L' subsection, armed with a Mark I 18/25-pounder gun, which was no more than a First World War 18-pdr bored out to take a heavier shell.

The Regiment left for France on 23 September 1939 as part of the British Expeditionary Force, expecting to reach Poland, which was being mauled by the German Panzer Divisions. Poland was the catalyst for entering the war, and in ignorance of intelligence to the contrary, we really thought that somehow we were Poland bound, but had no idea of how we were going to get there! It took a while to realize that this was not the case. Part I sets out my remembrance of that abortive campaign.

May 1940 to June 1944 was a time of training in England. I joined the newly formed 13th (HAC) Regiment, RHA in January 1941, being promoted in May 1942 to Warrant Officer Class II (Battery Sergeant Major, or BSM) in 'D' Troop, 'H' Battery. We were destined for North Africa in 1942, but it was cancelled at the last moment and we settled down, with new equipment and armaments, to train for Operation Overlord in June 1944.

Part II differs from Part I, in that it is more detailed. Although I took no notes of day-to-day activities, I had the good fortune in the 1970s to meet up with a man who was in the Battery Office at the time. He had typed up the daily notes recorded by Major Smythe-Osbourne MC (the Officer Commanding 'H' Battery) and had had the presence of mind to keep a copy, which he passed on to me. I have included a random page (see page 9), and these notes have enabled me to devise a chronological sequence of events around which I have woven my own experiences. My encounter with this ex-Battery Clerk was fleeting and I regret being unable to acknowledge the debt I owe him.

### Role

Sergeant majors are invariably caricatured in amusing scenarios as bawling idiots, as seen, for example, by Windsor Davies in the admirable TV series

# EXTRACTS FROM THE DAILY JOTTINGS OF A BATTERY CLERK

| June. | | **Cheux.** |
|---|---|---|

by M Tgt on same wood.  Panthers fished out of wood and Hill 112 taken.  Bty firing continuously.  L/Bdr Darragon, part of RD crew wounded by shell fire when Kinnersley and Gnr Clay wounded by mortar while mending it - evactd.  Ammunition expenditure approx 150 rpg.

29    0001-0600    Battery firing to cover withdrawal of 29 A.B.

**Norrey-en-Bessin.**

0630-2200    Bty leager for rest and maintenance, at 913707.

**St. Mavvier.**

2200-2359    Bty action 918694 supporting 15 Scottish Div.  Firing on DF and HF etc. tasks against Panzer counter attack on West Flank, Ammo expend 30 rpg.

30    Bty re-organised and firing various tasks in support of 15 Scottish and 53 Div.

1300    Bty lightly shelled by 105  No casualties.

July.    **S. Norrey-en-Bessin.**

1    1745    Position shelled by 105s.

1815    U Tgt stonk fired on 942622.  Amm expend 371 rounds.  Position and mortared intermittently during the evening.  Harrassing Fire Tasks shot.

2350    U Tgt Stonk shot scale 3.

2    a.m.    Position intermittently shelled.

1750    BC shoots 77 Med. Regt with success

2325    DF Task 170 fired at Scale IO.

3    0120    DF Task 174 fired 3 times.

1145    798 rounds ammo expenditure.

p.m.    Position heavily shelled - 5 light AA men wounded.

1805    Bty moved back 700 yards to near Pototenbessin as old position getting very hot.  New position 913711 DF Tasks during the night.

4    1130    Recce parties move to 9365.

**Mouen.**

1500    Bty moves to 9365 - No firing.

*It Ain't Half Hot, Mum,* and by Phil Silvers in *Bilko,* and whilst we in the RHA liked to do a bit of shouting now and then, we were not warrant officers for nothing.

The role of a WO2 in an armoured artillery formation has not, in my experience, been written down; it evolves from circumstances existing at the time. He is by no means a drill sergeant. That he is responsible to his Troop Commander for the discipline of the men means that he did it mostly by his personality and expressed military knowledge. He had to earn respect, particularly from his nine troop sergeants.[2] Not to do so made for an uncomfortable situation.

There are differences between the action roles of a Troop WOII in units comprised of towed guns (Field Artillery) and guns mounted on armoured tracked vehicles (quaintly called Horse Artillery). In the case of the former, his prime role in action was to ensure that the guns occupied positions that might already have been surveyed in, and to lead the towing vehicles back to some place at the rear called the Wagon Lines, then alternating between the two locations. In the latter case, that situation does not arise. Technical competence is required in military survey, mathematics, ballistics, a full range of gunnery detail and some knowledge of battle tactics, all with a keen eye for detail. In my own case, as the narrative will show, I was respectively Troop WOII, Troop Leader, Relief Gun Position Officer (GPO) and Forward Observation Officer (FOO). Admittedly, some of these duties arose from the exigencies of the moment, although the combined duties of Relief GPO, Troop Leader and Troop BSM existed on a permanent daily basis for eight months in 1944.

## Armament
In the brief twenty-day campaign in France and Belgium during May 1940, my Regiment (10th Field) was armed with 18/25 pdrs. Almost every part of its operation had to be manhandled by its team of six men, including the gun sergeant. During the brief campaign, my gun fired 317 shells, with 161 being fired in the first few hours.

Previous to the Part II campaign, the many training exercises showed that the tanks of an armoured division required close artillery support, but towed guns were unsuitable for this task. My regiment (13th (HAC) RHA)

---

2 Many years later, it was said of me at the time that the Troop was never sure whether I was being serious or joking, so to play safe they opted for the former. It made for a mutually comfortable relationship. From the time of being a raw recruit I had been nicknamed Pedro, and this stuck through my entire career.

was therefore converted to tracked and armoured vehicles on which were mounted the purpose-built 25-pdr Mark 2 gun, reputed to be the best gun ever made, with a range of 13,400 yards (7.6 miles). This self-propelled ensemble was named a 'Sexton', manned by six men, including the sergeant and the driver; its primary role called for it to accompany the tanks in battle.

## Outline

This memoir deals, therefore, with my battle experiences, first as a gun sergeant (Part I), and second as a Battery Sergeant Major (Part II). These battle experiences enabled me to command a gun in the face of the enemy and later to command four guns in action.

Part I tells the story of a campaign begun in high spirits, which rapidly turned sour in the face of a retreat and ultimate collapse. It was a time of utter confusion, with no one at my immediate level and below having the faintest idea of what was happening. The only good thing about it, as far as we were concerned, was that from the beginning to the end we remained a coherent, fully operational, troop ('C' Troop, 30/46 Battery), which made understanding of the chaos even more difficult. When we were in action (frequently) we fought like devils, day and night, and most of the time we had little sleep, no rest, and food rations dwindled to nil halfway through. My gun was constantly in action, firing over short ranges, and only when we had a direct hit which killed my second-in-command and wounded two others (myself included), did I report the sad words 'No. 1 gun out of action, sir'. As far as I am aware, there is little detailed reading on this abortive campaign.

Part II takes on a different approach, as illustrated at the beginning. It takes a chronological stance, around which I have set out the circumstances as I experienced them. I am no hero, but the exigencies of the many large and small battles (operations) often put me in positions in which I had to act beyond my normal roles. This memoir illuminates the point.

## Acknowledgements

As noted above, Part II owes its existence to the unknown Battery Clerk who kept a copy of the daily sequence of events. Elsewhere, if I refer to a source, I identify it in a footnote. Any errors and omissions, and there are probably many, are entirely my responsibility.

# Part 1

# Chapter 1

# The 'Phoney' Period, September 1939 to May 1940

—⁓—

A state of war was declared against Germany on 3 September 1939, and at that time I was a regular soldier, twenty-one years of age, and newly promoted from Lance Sergeant to full Gun Sergeant. My regiment was the 10th Field Regiment, Royal Artillery. I was posted to 'C' Troop, 30/46 Battery, commanding 'L' subsection of a 18/25-pdr gun and six men. The Regiment was mobilized for war in early August.

On Saturday, 23 September, the Regiment left its barracks at Deepcut, Surrey for the last time, marching in drill order to the small railway station at Frimley, en route to Southampton. In the evening, we sailed for Cherbourg, arriving early morning the next day, the 24th. We were on foot, while the guns and vehicles went separately from Barry (Cardiff) to St Nazaire.

A meal was available in the Cherbourg Fish Market, prepared by the advance party. An amusing incident took place there when some port official demanded that I append my signature to a document that authorised the requisitioning of the Market – I did so, on behalf of His Majesty the King! We were then allowed several hours to explore the town, where some of the men who had served time in India tried their smattering of Urdu on the French! At about eleven in the evening, we boarded a train (Third Class) that wound its way slowly through the French countryside to destinations unknown. In mid-afternoon of the 26th, we arrived at Salesme, from whence we marched some 5 or 6 kilometres in very hot weather, along a quiet country road, to the little village of Grez-en-Bouere, midway between Laval and Chateaugontier. Here, we were reunited with our guns and vehicles which had been driven from St Nazaire. This process of unification took about ten days, which suited me as, by some strange coincidence, this village was well known to me from pre-war 'back-pack' days.

In the early days of October, in indifferent weather, the Battery set off, fully equipped, to its action stations on the Franco-Belgian border. It took us four days to reach Landas, a nondescript village south of Lille, and my Troop ('C') was billeted in a Dutch barn, an agricultural structure which had only a roof supported by slender columns, with no side cladding. This cheerless abode coincided with a change in the weather, heralding one of the worst winters in living memory.

Together with the other three gun sergeants,[1] I brought my gun immediately into an action position alongside the embanked Lille-Charleroi railway line, facing east into Belgium (which was a neutral country at the time). Numbering from the right, I was No. 2 gun, hard by the level-crossing keeper's cottage. The ground was already waterlogged, so trying to dig gun pits was a continual nightmare. I would leave the position more or less dry at nightfall, but by the next morning it was in two feet of muddy water.

The cold wet weather grew progressively worse, so from November into the New Year the principal routine was simply to maintain the guns ready for action, resorting nightly to the chore of starting all engines every ten minutes to prevent them from freezing up.

Relief from these unwelcome chores came in January 1940 when the Battery was pulled out of the line to indulge in some mobile training in and around Bapaume on the Somme. The weather was appalling, with temperatures at midday being well below freezing point. This atrocious weather of snow, sleet and ice also prevented us from carrying out any of the planned mobile training, as the roads were choked with frozen snow.

This interlude was then interrupted very suddenly, as it was learned from captured documents that the Germans intended to invade Belgium on 17 January.[2] We had to make a hurried dash back to Landas to occupy the frozen gun pits so recently vacated. Fortunately, Hitler took alarm at the premature disclosure of his plans, and, combined with the chaotic weather, decided to postpone the invasion.

This scare meant the resumption of our grim and cheerless routine, but it did not last long as in mid-February we left Landas for a few days to go down to Sisonne in the vicinity of the famed Maginot Line. This barren

---

1 The batteries consisted of three troops, A, B and C in 30/46 Battery, and D, E and F in 51/54 Battery. Each troop had four 18/25-pdrs. Later, this was reorganized to form three batteries to a regiment, with each battery having two troops.

2 A German plane carrying an officer armed with these plans crashed on Belgian soil, causing the BEF to be put on full alert.

undulating area was the shooting ground of the French artillery regiments and we were able to fire (not in anger) our first shells on continental soil. On our return, staying for only a few days, we were again relieved and pleased to vacate our gun positions, proceeding to Varennes on the Somme for night training. We then returned to Bapaume, where, once more, our pleasant stay was interrupted when Hitler invaded Holland and Belgium on Friday, 10 May 1940. We thus made our way somewhat hurriedly back to Landas to make last-minute preparations, before proceeding into action. This was the start of our real war.

I make a break here to describe the manner in which we were armed. In the immediate pre-war years, we did not have a 'proper' gun. Political attitudes between the two wars had been largely pacifist and matters did not improve until the advent of Adolf Hitler in 1933. Even so, by the time war broke out, research and development into military equipment had barely reached the mass-production stage, especially in artillery and tanks. What we did have – and we were thought to be the most experienced Field Regiment in the Royal Artillery – was a converted 18-pdr gun of the type that was used extensively in the First World War. Pneumatic tyres replaced the old cartwheels and the barrel was bored out to accept the new 25-pdr shell, but all else, more or less, was retained. A First World War gunner would have felt quite at home with it.

This gun became the 18/25-pdr Mk1, with a maximum range of 11,800 yards (6.75 miles). It fired a shell weighing 25 lb, propelled by a charge that could be varied according to the range and type of target. In transit, the gun was hooked on to a limber that carried a stock of shells, which in turn hooked on to an articulated six-wheeled tractor that also carried the gun crew and the essential stores. The gun crew comprised seven men, including the driver and the sergeant commanding it.[3]

That Friday and Saturday were spent ensuring that we were fully armed, fuelled and ready for action. Personal kit was packed, and stored away in whatever crevices were available in the tractors and on the guns. We barely slept that night, which was a forerunner of what was to come.

---

3 For a fascinating account of these matters, see Bidwell, Shelford, *Gunners at War*, Arrow Books, 1972.

# Chapter 2

# The Battle, May 1940

—⁄⁄⁄—

Our battle began on Saturday, 11 May; it was warm and pleasant and we were full of excitement. We left Landas for a destination in Belgium, but I did not know where. It was late in the evening when the journey ended in the great forest south-east of Brussels, known as Foret de Soignes, where we rested for the night in the shelter of the trees, except for a reconnaissance party going forward to reconnoitre gun positions. The next day, Sunday, 'C' Troop moved off early to occupy the chosen positions. These were in open, rolling pasture fields, a mile or so west of the River Dyle, in which, on Sunday and Monday, we dug gun pits in the regulation style and were inspected by officers in the manner of a peacetime Saturday morning parade. I was No. 4 gun on the left of the Troop, with the other three spread out to my right at about 25-yard intervals.

The weather was brilliant, hot and sunny, and almost everyone was stripped to the waist, glistening with perspiration. Then, early on the Tuesday morning, 14 May, the war really began. Once we started firing, there was no let-up, and in about five hours my gun alone fired 161 shells at an average rate of roughly one every two minutes. In between this bombardment, the gun barrel became so hot that it was unsafe to fire, and on several occasions I had to report my gun temporarily out of action.

It was in this, our first position, that our Regimental Commander, Colonel Parham, created a record of firing all twenty-four guns through the medium of a wireless net, a procedure that had not been used before. His target was a stationary group of German tanks in the act of refuelling.[1] We all cheered when we were told about it.

It was late in the afternoon of Tuesday that we heard the disquieting news over the wireless that not only was the enemy attacking in front of us, but also they were advancing miles behind us. We could hardly believe our

---

1 See Bidwell, *Gunners at War*, p. 135.

ears and were inclined to dismiss it as enemy propaganda, especially as we seemed to be doing so well in holding the Germans on the Dyle. I learned later that the French Army on our right was falling back, leaving us with exposed flanks.

Shortly after hearing this unwelcome news, we received the order 'Prepare to Move', and as I still had an unfired shell in the breech, I cocked up the barrel to maximum elevation and range (about 6 miles) and emptied the gun accordingly. Where the shell went, I do not know. Driver Foxwell brought up the tractor and we scrambled aboard, leaving behind the usual debris of spent cartridge cases, ammunition and ration boxes. Someone was shouting, 'Get the Hell out of it as quick as you can.' By this time we needed no bidding, and went! I was not to know that this was actually the beginning of the Great Retreat that terminated on the Dunkirk beaches.

In this action I had been No. 4 gun, but because of the configuration of the gun position I was the first to leave, the others trailing behind me. I tucked in behind the Troop Leader's 15cwt Personnel/Utility truck, occupied, I think, by our Troop Commander, Captain Peter Riddell. We travelled back through the Foret de Soignies, then north-west through the southern suburbs of Brussels, passing, about midnight of the 14th/15th, through the Grande Place without seeing a soul. It was a ghostly sight. Normally it would be crowded with people and even during the night there would be considerable activity, but not tonight. It was dark and silent, even sinister. With the exception of Driver Foxwell and myself, the rest of the crew were asleep in their seats We were now driving towards Ninove on the River Dendre and at dawn took up several action stations, staying only for a brief time in each, but events all around were moving too fast and we did not get the opportunity to fire.

The situation was becoming more confused by the hour, but eventually, on Wednesday, 15 May, in the morning, we came to a small village called Eyseringen, which we entered over a railway level crossing, before nosing our way along the village street. Suddenly, a hail of machine-gun bullets were fired in our direction, with one or two ripping into the canvas roof of my tractor a couple of feet from my head. I was standing up at the time, with both hands gripping the top of the windscreen, but there was no point in doing anything as the tractor offered neither shelter nor safety. The gunners in the seats behind me never woke so quickly! The Troop Leader was in front and I was immediately behind him. I couldn't at first locate the source of the firing, until I saw the outline of German tanks to our left front. We were well and truly ambushed! To go forward was out of the question and for a few moments the Troop column halted.

Captain Riddell remained cool, and, seeing a small residential road on his right, he led us into it, not only to provide temporary shelter from the raking machine-gun fire, but also to find a way out of the village. Unfortunately, this narrow residential road turned out to be a cul-de-sac, with a high wall barring our way, and there was nothing for it but to turn the column round and run the gauntlet of the German fire. This was easier said than done. A gun-towing tractor, with a limber full of high-explosive shells, attached to which is an 18/25-pdr gun, has an articulated length of over 30 feet. Thus, the three separate units had to be unhooked and manhandled with the aid of the tractor; since the gun teams were nose to tail and the road narrow, the confusion was acute. Somehow, we all managed to get sorted out, fully expecting an enemy tank to site itself at the junction of the small road and the road through the village. The way, however, was momentarily clear.

The drivers trod hard on the accelerators and we screeched round the corner that headed back towards the level crossing. Alas, escape seemed not to be, as on the other side of the crossing lurked another enemy Mk III tank astride the road. Captain Riddell, resourceful as always, on reaching the level crossing ordered his driver to turn left and to drive the 15cwt truck along the railway lines. We followed suit. It was an extraordinary experience – the nearside wheels (right-hand drive) were on the outside of the railway lines and on the edges of the sleepers; the offside wheels ran on the sleepers between the tracks. It was a nightmare for the drivers: the steering wheels bucked and jerked in their hands; nor could they keep steady engine revolutions, because it was difficult for them to maintain sensitive contact with the accelerators. The guns and limbers swayed from side to side, bumping up and down. Everything that could fall off did so. It was too much for one of the guns which broke loose and we all had to halt to allow the gun to be manhandled back on to the railway tracks. It is a cardinal principle in the artillery that one never abandons a gun. It was unthinkable to leave it, so we all lent our efforts to get the gun back on the railway track.

We were successful in escaping from the ambush and free of being fired upon. But where were we going and how were we to get off the railway lines? As far ahead as we could see, the rail track seemed endless. We covered several kilometres in this way before we found a welcome level crossing at some village that did not seem to be in enemy hands. As the Troop Leader set off to the south-west, I wondered if even he had the slightest idea where he was heading. Fortunately we were still in wireless contact with the rest of the Battery, wherever they might be, as a result of which we came into action somewhere in the Ninove-Enghien-Gramont triangle. There we fired off a few rounds at targets unknown to us, but it helped to relieve the tension.

# Chapter 3

# A Strange Adventure

—⚡—

As darkness fell we took advantage of it to get a few hours sleep to recharge our exhausted, battered and bruised bodies. We bedded down as best we could, with no thought of divesting any clothes. Just after midnight, on Thursday, 16 May, a hand shook me by the shoulder and someone woke me in a whisper, ordering me to keep quiet and to follow him. I recognized him to be the Battery Captain and he urged upon me complete silence. He gave me no time to tell my gunners that I was required elsewhere. I followed him to a waiting 15cwt P/U truck, with its driver hunched up in the seat.

I climbed into the back of the truck without the faintest idea of what was happening. No explanation was forthcoming until much later (when I learned that the Allied front was broken, and that the Germans were pouring through, leaving our right flank totally exposed). There I sat, surrounded by half a dozen four-gallon tins of petrol. We sped off into the dark night. A couple of hours later, having travelled over roads choked with fleeing refugees, groups of dejected French soldiers and vehicles of all kinds, we came to a built-up area that was either Santbergen or Gramont. The night was still dark, with no moon, the darkness only mitigated by the flashes of distant gunfire mirrored on the clouds and myriads of coloured Very lights put up by the enemy. I was never able to decipher them.

The built-up area around us was crowded with families and individuals of all sorts carrying their precious belongings in prams, on bicycles, horses and carts, or simply on their backs. Women were weeping, caring for frightened children, whilst the men seemed to be running hither and thither for no obvious purpose. We were held up by the noisy crowd at this road junction, unable to move forward. It was a pitiful and worrying sight, which to me was made worse by having no idea of what we were doing. All I knew at that point was that we seemed to be fighting a rearguard action, but the situation seemed to be much more sinister. Machine-gun fire sounded in the distance, and occasional sheets of white light lit up the horizon caused by the Germans firing into places where it would add to the hysteria of the inhabitants and refugees. The whole scene was unreal, but it had a dangerous reality.

In the midst of trying to force our way through this throng, we were accosted by a plump Belgian gentleman, still formally dressed in a sharp pinstriped suit now sorely ruffled. He stood by an expensive limousine, accommodating a number of people, including children. He waved his arms in a distracted manner, clutching a large wad of banknotes. He explained, with many gesticulations, that he had run out of petrol, and begged the Battery Captain for a supply, in return for which he could name his own price. To my disquiet, the Battery Captain was sufficiently moved to hand over one of our four-gallon tins, ignoring the offer of payment. Whatever we were up to, I thought that our need for petrol might become urgent, hoping that the Captain's generosity would not jeopardize whatever mission we were on.

Eventually, with the Captain at the wheel and the exhausted driver asleep in his seat, we were able to force a passage through the milling crowd, getting through into Gramont itself. The road in front of us ran downhill towards a bridge over the Dendre Canal. As we approached the bridge, a burly soldier barred our path. He was either a Royal Engineer or a Military Policeman, and he seemed determined not to let us pass. His message to the irate Captain was clear. 'Can't go over the bridge, mate. We're just going to blow it.' The Captain, without saying a word, trod hard on the accelerator and with tyres screaming, set off at speed towards the bridge, almost throwing me out of the open end of the vehicle. It took but a few moments to reach the bridge and then we were over on the other side, but only just. There was a huge explosion and the bridge collapsed, covering us in debris and dust. Had the Captain not been driving, the brief time it would have taken to give orders to the driver, and for the sleepy driver to comply, would have put us in the middle of the bridge as it went up. And that would have been the end of the war for us. So we had the doubtful honour of being the last over the doomed Pont de Gramont, but it also denied passage to the crowd of refugees entrapped on the other side, and to anyone else following on.

The Battery Captain was still too intent on picking his way over country roads and thrusting his way through the groups of fleeing refugees to be communicative. He had barely said a word since the journey began, and I still had no inkling of what we were doing, or where we were going. After a short while, as dawn broke on the 16th, we drove off the road into the yard of a group of small buildings. I followed the Captain as he walked towards a cottage. The door was unlocked and we entered. A very old man, sleeping on a ragged sofa, awakened with a look of shocked surprise, probably never having seen a British soldier since 1918. I had the feeling that he thought we were going to shoot him!

Gradually, with the Captain loosening up a little, and no doubt feeling that some explanation was due, he gave me some idea of our mission. The British Army, it seemed, was in full retreat, and it was not to be talked about in case it weakened morale. So that was the need for secrecy. The Captain's orders were to find a place, out of enemy reach, where we could regroup. Our Regiment was fragmented and the divisional infantry were in some disarray. Once a suitable place was found, my job was to remain there on guard while the Captain returned to some arranged rendezvous, to lead the Battery in.

We moved off, leaving a very frightened old man to gather his senses, and a short time later, probably about four or five o'clock in the morning, we came across a sign pointing to a monastery. We turned into the long driveway, stopping in a quadrangle of institutional buildings. A dignified nun, who turned out to be the Mother Superior, enquired what we were doing there. The Captain explained in halting French that he wished to bring in some soldiers in need of a short rest. After some further explanation, she offered us full support, marshalling her flock of Pious Sisters accordingly. The Captain, after giving me certain orders, sped off, although I did wonder how he was getting back, and to where? Apparently I was left there to prevent any other unit getting there before us, to act as a guide when the Battery arrived and to liaise with the Mother Superior.

After chatting with the Mother Superior, who, surprisingly, spoke very good English, I retraced my lonely steps back to the main road, not at all happy. It was just getting light and there was not a soul in sight. I felt completely abandoned, as I had no conviction of ever seeing the Regiment again. So much could happen in so short a time. I could hear distant gunfire and the staccato sounds of machine guns, which seemed to be getting closer – or was it my imagination? I was hungry, thirsty and tired out. I sat on the side of the road, leaning against a brick wall. The dawn was cold and grey, and I walked up and down to restore circulation, feeling very miserable.

At last I heard the sound of approaching vehicles. Unsure whether they were friendly or hostile, I stood my ground. I was relieved, therefore, to see my Battery Commander, Major Croker-Barrington, standing up in the front of a truck at the head of my Troop. I was pleased to be reunited with my gun crew, who held the firm belief that I had deserted them in the middle of the night! Indeed, I believe I was reported missing, but the Captain was able to explain differently. The tired old saying 'nothing ever goes according to plan' was certainly true in this case, for instead of intending to spend a day or two days there, we only lasted a couple of hours, as the Germans were dangerously close.

# Chapter 4

# Retreat

—⟋ᵚᚚ⟍—

During our short stay at the monastery, we were able to manage, before setting off again, a certain amount of personnel reorganization, and some essential maintenance of guns and vehicles. Very few of us knew that we were in full retreat and those who did found it very disquieting. Most of the men thought we were still chasing the Germans! We had come some 80 miles from our original position on the River Dyle, with little food or sleep, and it was now Friday, 17 May. We did not know that Brussels had surrendered to the Germans that day.

The two days of the 17th and 18th were spent moving westwards, and even coming into action a few times to fire off a few rounds. We eventually made our tortuous way to Tournai, where we were expected to make a stand on the River Escaut – our second main action (the first being on the Dyle). Our task was to support the Cameron Highlanders[1] in defending the bridge over the river. We soon came under fire ourselves from German 75mm guns and mortars, but fortunately for us, the marauding enemy was not able to keep in touch with their own heavier artillery, most of which was still horse drawn, and lagged far behind the enemy tanks and infantry.

Our gun position on Saturday, 18 May was in some allotments at the rear of houses fronting a street in Tournai that led down to the Escaut. We were firing parallel to the street. The weather was warm, dry and sunny, and we shed clothing to make the work of servicing the guns more comfortable. A strange incident then occurred for which I have no explanation. Close by my gun, to my front, was a post and wire fence, upon which I hung my battledress blouse. As our firing became more intense, the Germans reciprocated to the full, their high-explosive shells and airbursts falling all around us. We knew we were being observed but we did not know how or where from. As the firing on both sides slowed down considerably,

---

1 An infantry regiment in the 2nd Infantry Division to which we ourselves belonged.

I was able to regain possession of my blouse. It was not until I donned it that I discovered that the button flaps of my two breast pockets had been severed as if with a razor blade. The rest of the tunic was neither damaged nor scorched. How this could have happened, I have no idea. It would not be impossible to deduce that the tabs had been removed some time earlier whilst I was actually wearing the blouse, as I had been battered and knocked about by shell blasts on several occasions.

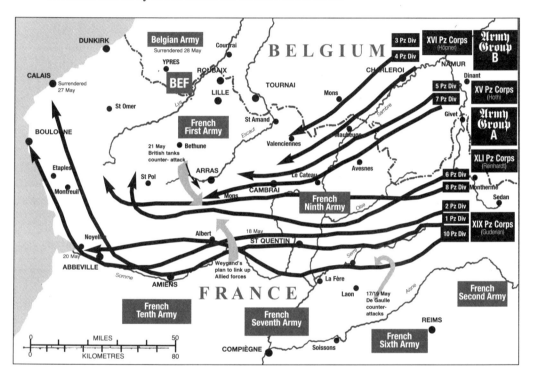

German advance to the Channel, May 1940. (*Courtesy of Patrick Wilson*)

During this lull in the action I ventured, for some reason or other, into the street which led down to the river, keeping a wary eye on what was happening around me. We had been told that a lunatic asylum had been opened up, releasing several hundred inmates, and we wished to be clear of them. I passed by a few shops that were empty of people, but still showing their wares. I could have helped myself to jewellery, clothing and even the contents of a butcher's shop, but the fear of the death penalty for looting persisted in my mind, and I did not wish to be any part of it. The duel between the Germans and us flared up again, particularly as most of theirs were airbursts, which we did not like. Then I heard the order 'Take Post', and I had to race back to my gun, which alone fired over a hundred shells (the equivalent to a ton of high explosive). But it was to no avail, as the Germans forced the Highlanders off the bridge in a fierce bayonet duel, causing us to evacuate our position rather quickly.

We retired westwards to the Franco-Belgian border in the vicinity of Campin north of Carvin, from where we had begun our war what now seemed to be ages before. Someone told me that the Germans were 40 miles *behind* our right flank! It was all very puzzling and I only hoped that someone higher up was doing something about it. At Carvin, on Sunday, 19 May, we occupied gun pits that had been dug by our contemporaries in the 'phoney' months previously, but did not stay there for long as the Germans, who had now forced a crossing of the Escaut, nearly caught up with us. This time we moved south-westwards towards Seclin, where we engaged in trying, unsuccessfully, to keep the enemy at bay.

From there, we moved on the 20th to La Bassée in First World War country, and wondered why we were firing due west into Bethune? Surely we should be facing east from where the Germans were debouching? We did not know until much later that Generals Guderian and Rommel were on their way to the Channel ports, and that the BEF was encircled. As a result, we moved on Tuesday morning, the 21st, to Laventie on the La Bassée Canal, where we undertook our third main action (after Dyle and Escaut), a position that needs to be described in some detail.

The immediate countryside was more or less open and lay within the coalfields of north-eastern France. In this latest gun position, I was the No. 1, or right-hand gun of the Troop. The other guns were away to my left at staggered intervals with about 25 yards between them. I was sited a few yards away from the country road that stretched in a straight line in front of me, the same direction in which my gun was laid. Separating the gun pit from the road was a drainage ditch. Ahead, a lone cottage stood by the road about 300 yards to my front, and beyond that, about a mile or so away, loomed a spoil tip belonging to the nearby colliery. Behind my gun pit were the assorted buildings of a farm that was still occupied by an ailing old lady, tended by a young girl.

By now we had been in action against the enemy almost continuously for eight days and nights. None of us had had much sleep, and rations were scarce and irregular. Hunger and thirst made the men irritable, so we searched the farm for something to eat and drink, with the officers turning a blind eye. To make matters worse, the weather broke that evening, with low cloud cover and drizzling rain. We began firing almost immediately upon occupation, at ranges of 2,000-2,500 yards, the shells bursting on or beyond the spoil tip.[2] We had dug shallow gun pits, but the ground quickly became waterlogged due to surface water run-off. The result of this was that the force of the recoil of the barrel on firing dragged the gun carriage backwards several feet, so that each time the gun fired it had to be manhandled back and relaid. It was hard work.

During the night of 21/22 May, a violent thunderstorm added to the misery of this position, especially as the enemy persisted in lobbing a few shells over at random times. I managed to sleep for an hour or so by lying on the rain-sodden ground. When I woke, I saw that a shell splinter had neatly punctured my steel helmet which lay by my side.

The Germans were not repulsed to any extent in this locality and they gained a foothold on the spoil tip in front of me, establishing an observation post. This was most unfortunate, for the lie of the land was such that, of all the guns in the Troop, mine was the only one that could be observed by the enemy. For a while, we were shelled in a desultory sort of manner, to which we responded, but ammunition was now running low, with little hope of replenishment. It was obvious that the German observer was trying to pinpoint me, but he was either lackadaisical about it, or was otherwise engaged, for his shooting was erratic. One or more shells, however, hit the lone cottage to my front, causing it to burst into flames, with smoke obliterating our gun-aiming points. This sort of unpredicted shelling continued over into Thursday, 23 May.

The German observer must have applied himself at last to the task of putting us out of action, because the shelling became more intense, bursting unpleasantly close. We feared the worst. Sooner or later, we would almost certainly be blasted out of existence, but we had to keep on firing and stick it out. A shell exploded a few yards in front of the gun, throwing up debris that covered us in muck and damaged the gun shield. There could be no thought of taking cover, even though the shelling became more persistent. One shell almost scored a direct hit as it exploded just in front of the gun. This was followed by another shell that landed even nearer,

---

2 A 18/25-pdr was a gun howitzer, so it could lob a shell in a high arc as well a firing at a low trajectory. Changes of varying propellants were used to make both functions possible.

rocking the gun back on its spade and throwing us all to the ground. The rubber tyres of the gun wheels were shredded. The acrid smoke, searing the throat and irritating the eyes, added to the bruising and battering. Even so, we recovered ourselves and kept the gun firing as best we could. A third shell exploded in more or less the same place, this time, in addition to knocking us over, it damaged the glass inspection window of the hydraulic recoil system, so allowing oil to escape. This was serious, because the gun could not fire with the barrel recoil system out of action.

Gunner Hopkins, the gun loader, came to the rescue. He was a die-hard Welsh docker, with a dark sense of humour, usually applied to anyone in authority. On this occasion, however, acting on his own initiative, he ran back to the farmhouse, under shellfire, returning triumphantly waving a flat cork of the type used to seal a pickle jar. It fitted perfectly into the glass aperture. I topped up the recoil system with spare oil kept for such happenings and the gun was brought back into action.

The German observer kept up his onslaught, banging shells all around us, until the inevitable happened. We took an almost direct hit. It exploded only a yard or two to the right of the gun. Once more, we were blown off our feet, but this time fatally so. Bombardier Tom Cutler, who was my No. 2, had his back blown away. Gunner Searle, who was my No. 3 gun layer, was wounded in the right arm, and I was wounded in the right leg. Incredibly, after some clearing up, and attending to Tom's dying moments, we were ordered to resume firing, ignoring our wounds. Indeed, I did not know for a short time that I had been wounded, because a shell splinter is still red hot as it punctures flesh and bone, so cauterizing the wound and briefly nullifying the pain.

Bursting shells were now smothering the whole gun position, as the German observer felt he had got the range right. Conditions were untenable, but although the situation was acutely serious, we had to keep at it. This could not last long, however, and at last the Troop Sergeant Major rushed among the guns, shouting to us to 'Cease Fire and Limber Up', adding that we only had seven minutes to get out. I do not know on what intelligence this precise timing was calculated, but its import was clear. My towing tractor, also damaged by the shelling, but still moderately serviceable, came up from the Wagon Lines behind the farm buildings. We clambered aboard, relieved to see that, at the same time, someone was seeing to Tom Cutler's body. As we moved off apace, I could see German infantry movements to our rear.

I took stock of my situation. I had lost two men (Cutler and Searle), there were no tyres on the gun wheels, the dial sight was damaged and my own wound was beginning to bleed. To make matters worse, the tractor's auto-vac system that supplied the engine with petrol was damaged, and needed periodic filling by hand.

## Chapter 5

# A Tortuous Journey

—⚭—

We set off, therefore, in the late afternoon of Thursday, 23 May, travelling northwards, my tyre-less gun wheels shedding sparks on the cobbled roads. We crossed the La Bassée Canal and bypassed Armentières, where we witnessed German Stuka dive-bombers obliterating parts of the town, which were blazing furiously. When we went into action south of the village of Watou, the food situation had by then become critical – we had had no rations for three days. Finally, an officer read out a proclamation that looting for food would no longer constitute a military offence.

In this context, we somehow learned that the NAAFI depot in Armentières had been bombed and abandoned, so a bombardier was despatched with a 15cwt truck to see what food he could salvage. His return was awaited with mouth-watering expectation, but he was away quite a long time, returning well into the evening having been held up by the chaos on the roads. We gathered round to see what he had managed to procure. Imagine our disappointment and anger to discover that the most he was able to collect were boxes of Duncan's Chocolate Bars and jars of Brylcream! His explanation, though perfectly valid, did nothing to assuage our need for food.

The food situation then tended to take precedence over fighting the Germans, as some of the men were feeling ill with hunger and no sleep. There were some farm buildings nearby, and men were despatched to see what they could find. Alas, there were no available foodstuffs to be found, the farm having already been ransacked, probably by refugees. They did, however, locate a pig and some chickens, but there was nothing we could do for the moment, as we were called upon for another fire mission.

This situation continued throughout the night of 24/25 May, but as dawn broke we resumed our quest for food, having made ourselves sick on chocolate bars! A so-called butcher was identified in the Troop, who attempted to slaughter the pig, but his efforts came to nought as the beast refused the offer of extinction. This left only the chickens, which were plucked and put in a pot, along with a few mouldy potatoes we found lying about. The menu was expected to be chicken stew.

Whilst all these culinary operations were being undertaken, the situation allowed me the opportunity to do something about my tyre-less gun wheels. Somewhere along the way I had acquired another limber, a two-wheeled box carrying ammunition. We therefore exchanged the wheels of the gun with those of the limber, which was abandoned. It was a relief to me to be reasonably mobile again.

We fired a few rounds here and there throughout the next day, Sunday the 26th, but as we were kept permanently on the alert we could not attend to the food situation; neither could we spare men from the guns to do something about it. With my gun team reduced from six to three, it was hard work keeping up a decent firing rate. My leg wound was also becoming troublesome.

We seemed to be living in a chaotic world where everything appeared to be unreal. Towns and villages were deserted and country roads were choked with people on the move. Our own routine consisted of moving from one place to another for no apparent reason. No sooner had we come into action positions than we had to pack up and move on, so close were the enemy on our heels. Fear was the order of the day for everybody, and not knowing the purpose of it all made matters even more incomprehensible. We did not know, for example, that the infantry division, of which we were a part, had literally ceased to exist, having been destroyed in the Béthune trap. It was now obvious to all that we were on the run – but where to? This soon became clear.

We had to leave Watou in a hurry in the evening of Monday the 27th, thereby abandoning the chicken stew which had been cooking for hours. The ground in front rose gently to the skyline, then dropped away. To get on to the main road that led through Watou, we had to follow a track that led towards the ridge in front, over which ground, we were told, German tanks were approaching. It was a race to see who got to the main road first. Fortunately, we won.

As we drove through the village, the scenes of carnage were indescribable. It had recently been dive-bombed and the dead, civilians and soldiers alike, lay everywhere. The enemy's air action was widespread, as we could see Stukas attacking Cassel and Hazebrouck in front.

31

By now it was dark and variously coloured Very lights, put up by the advancing Germans, illuminated the lowering sky. Machine-gun fire could be heard close by, as could various bangs and explosions. The sounds were all around us and there seemed to be no order to it all. The roads resembled a nightmare. Abandoned army trucks and guns lay nose to tail, with more littering the fields lining the roads; many of these vehicles were on fire. Soldiers from a variety of units shambled their way on foot, mingling with civilian refugees who seemed to be in a state of permanent hysteria. We, on the other hand, dishevelled as we were in every respect, were still an ordered, cohesive unit, with a full complement of guns and vehicles, but not of men. Had we again been called upon to come into action, we could have done, but for us the fighting was over for there were no Forward Observation Officers to give us orders. We were now being led, if that is the right word for easing one's way past debris of all kinds, by a young Lieutenant unknown to us, and we made slow progress through a night of indescribable confusion.

On the morning of Tuesday, 28 May, word trickled down from somewhere that we were bound for Dunkirk, from where we would be taken by ship to Le Havre or Dieppe to reform and join in the war again. The young Lieutenant leading us seemed to be a resourceful chap, for seeing a turning off to the right where conditions were not so bad, he turned us into it and we drove against the grain of the main exodus. I deduced from my map reading that we were heading for Bergues and this proved to be correct. I now know that we were among the outer defences of Dunkerque, but at the time this was not apparent. We skirted Bergues as we thought it might be occupied by Germans and came to a canal where we halted for a few hours. Incredibly, for we had forsaken the matter of food, someone brought around bully beef sandwiches, cut like doorsteps. During this pause, a reconnaissance was made to find a bridge to take us across the canal. This proved to be successful, for a rickety bridge of sorts was discovered at Warhem, over which we drove. It was now the middle of the night of 28/29 May, and at last we seemed to be free of the headlong rush that had previously held us up.

We were now heading for Dunkirk, but once more we had to join in with the general melee of packed roads, abandoned equipment and refugees. Miraculously, we still held together as a military unit. Eventually, we arrived at the coast at Malo-les-Bains early on the morning of Wednesday, 29 May, and we made our way to the small promenade that fronted on to the dunes. Our orders were to destroy all equipment that could be put to use by the Germans. Our usual method of putting a gun out of action was to ram in a shell at both ends of the barrel, retreat and pull the firing lever by using a long rope. The place was too crowded to engage in such activities. I removed from the gun all the parts needed to fire it, including the precious dial sight, the sight clinometer and the firing mechanism. I found it difficult to part with the rammer that I used to load the shell into the breach, so I brought it back with me as well – it is lying before me as I type this account. It had done its work well for I made a note at the time that, during the whole campaign lasting fifteen days and nights, my gun had fired 317 shells – 3½ tons of high explosive.

To carry these bits of hardware was not an easy task, especially as the wound in my right leg was becoming more troublesome. It was not life-threatening but I found that as I took a step forward it bled rather badly, so that my trouser leg was more red than khaki. So here I was, festooned with bits and pieces, but unable to walk. I sat down on a low wall feeling very miserable. The Troop had dispersed by now and I felt alone in the middle of the crowd. Relief, however, came in the shape of an unknown medical orderly who someone had directed to me. I tried to explain my plight but I was now light-headed and probably not very coherent. The loss of blood, coupled with general exhaustion and ebbing strength, was taking its toll. I think I passed out for I remember being laid on a stretcher – but very little else, except being on the sand dunes with bombs exploding nearby. My ears began to bleed.

I vaguely remember being hauled aboard a ship[1] that was moored alongside the Mole, and of being taken down below decks and propped up against a column, but how, I cannot recall. At around that time the ship was bombed and I do remember that the column on which I was leaning was bent forward by the bombing, causing me to be jack-knifed. Things thereafter became even more of a jumble.

When it was known we were heading for the French coast, it was generally thought that we would be taken further down the coast to Dieppe or Le Havre, reform and refit, and rejoin the war. Once the ship had docked at Dover, where signs are bi-lingual, I remember being put on a train on some sort of seat, and asked a lady, who was handing out mugs of tea, which of the two French ports we were at. I think I also enquired what an

---

1 I discovered later that it was the channel ferry, the SS *Canterbury*, which I believe was later sunk.

English-speaking lady was doing on a train in France. This confused scenario buzzed around in my mind as the train trundled through the night of 30 May in the direction of Wiltshire. I somehow found myself in Tidworth Military Hospital, where I was placed on a hospital trolley and operated on by a doctor and an Irish nurse. Between them they managed to extract a jagged piece of Krupp metal from my leg. After it was over, I was handed a piece of paper on which the doctor had pencilled 'Give this man 3,000 ATS.' I thought, What? In my state?[2]

That was the end of my first taste of war in face of the enemy; it was to be four more years before it happened again. Those four years were spent joining a newly formed regiment, 13th (HAC) Regiment, RHA, and training, first for North Africa, for which, in the event, we were not wanted, and then for the campaign in Normandy and beyond.

---

2 This was a shorthand note that might have read 3,000cc Anti Tetanus Solution. ATS was the Women's Auxiliary Territorial Service!

# Part 2

*Chapter 6*

# Enter Normandy

—\~~~—

O n the morning of Tuesday, 6 June 1944, I heard the news over the
BBC that Allied forces had landed in France to open the long-
awaited Second Front. Although it was no surprise that such a
momentous event was taking place, nevertheless it came as something of a
shock that it had actually happened at long last. At my level, as a Warrant
Officer II (Battery Sergeant Major) of 'D' Troop ('H' Battery, 13th (HAC)
Regiment RHA), I was not privy to any of the plans that were likely to
affect us, and I had little idea of the unfolding events. All I knew was that
the time had come at last, and the waiting was over.

My Troop, 'D' (known as 'Don'), was fully prepared for it. For weeks,
from when the Regiment arrived in Aldershot from Kilham in East
Yorkshire in early May, our guns and equipment had been fully armed,
fuelled and maintained to the extent that there was absolutely nothing left for
me to do. I was, in fact, for a few weeks a temporarily unemployed soldier.
The exceptions to unemployment were those officers who were seemingly
secretly briefed each day on forthcoming events. My Troop was trained to
the highest pitch, but now the time had come to put everything into motion.

The next day, 'Liberation Money' was issued – 30 French francs, I
believe. So far, so good. It clearly meant that we were off to France, and the
excitement mounted. Without any formal orders the men repeatedly went
over their guns, vehicles and personal equipment just in case something
might have been forgotten. Petrol tanks were filled to the top and ingenious
ways were devised to carry more in jerrycans strapped to the outside of the
self-propelled 'Sextons'.[1] Ammunition was checked and rechecked (the
Sexton carried sixty 25-pdr shells and cartridges); waterproofing shields

---

1 'Sexton' was the name given to the self-propelled 25-pdr Mk II gun. It was a Canadian RAM tank with
the top taken off to allow a 25-pdr to be installed. The tank had a Continental Radial air-cooled 9-cylinder
petrol engine developing 400 bhp, and could travel 125 miles (200 km) on full tanks, with a road speed of 25
mph (40.2 kph). It weighed 23.2 tons and carried a gun team of six men. In addition to the 25-pdr, it had
mountings for two 0.30 Browning machine guns, which I replaced with the larger 0.50 Brownings.

were anxiously inspected to see that they were properly in place in case we had a wet landing on the beaches; anything else that could be double-checked was.

Thursday the 8th and Friday the 9th passed in a euphoria of excitement and apprehension, and it was not until late on Friday that I was told we were to leave Aldershot on Sunday morning, 11 June, destination unknown (to us at Troop level). We travelled triumphantly through the northern suburbs of London, with people turning out to wave us on, and at 1645 hrs arrived at a secret camp in Little Warley in Essex, where the Regiment was incarcerated in tents to await embarkation at some unknown date. We had no tasks to perform and all the officers seemed to be employed elsewhere. Last-minute letters were written.

It was there that I had to organize a procedure called 'enforced rest'. You couldn't order men to go to sleep, nature is not like that, but you can order men to lie back and relax without fear of being accused of any dereliction of duty. Rest was essential to enable the body to build up and maintain the energy required to operate in conditions where there was little opportunity for rest. I became very keen on this procedure, and used it time and time again in the months to come, particularly in my own case where, according to the exigencies of the day, I had to perform four jobs at various times throughout a 24 hour day.[2] Because of my frequent catnaps in lieu of a night's sleep I was called Rip Van Winkle (but not to my face!).

We stayed in this tented camp throughout Sunday and Monday, cut off from the outside world until early on Tuesday, 13 June, when the long-awaited order came to 'Prepare to Move'. Our immediate destination was Tilbury Docks where the Regiment and its vehicles and equipment were loaded on to LST51 (Landing Ship Tank, No. 51), which sailed at 1245 hrs. LSTs were the naval equivalent of today's Channel ferries. It had two main decks, the lower one of which accommodated the tanks and self-propelled guns, with the ramp closing up behind them, and an upper deck that carried the soft-skinned vehicles and men's accommodation. There was also the usual variety of galleries, dining rooms and so on. LST51 was an American-built boat and it had an American crew. Travel by LST was no relaxing affair and it was believed by those who sailed in her that it had a capacity for rolling in all ways at the same time. This apt description was soon to be put to the test. The weather was uncertain, the sky cloudy and sullen; I was

---

2 Troop Sergeant Major, Acting Troop Leader, Relief Gun Position Officer and Forward Observation Officer.

unaware that the bad weather had caused D-Day to be postponed for twenty-four hours. The sea was choppy as we set sail into the unknown.

As we gained the open sea, the ship began to pitch and roll in an alarming manner. It was a combination of this lurching and the American food that caused gastronomical problems among many of the men. Immediately we settled on board, the generous Americans plied us with food, the likes of which we had not seen since 1939. The portions of an American breakfast for one man would have fed six of us back in England – and we were unaccustomed to having what appeared to be treacle on pancakes mixed up with the bacon and eggs. Within a short time of dining, some men's faces assumed a greenish colour as internal parts of the body grievously revolted against an unaccustomed menu, and men were compelled to race for the rails to soil the rolling waves of the English Channel.

Meanwhile, there developed a matter of some considerable concern. Some unusual noises emanated from the lower tank deck and some of the American crew were seen running around in a rather distracted manner. To find out what was going on, I made my way down the iron gangway leading to the lower tank deck and gazed with alarm at the scene. The eccentric wallowing of the ship had caused some of the tanks and guns to break loose from their deck chains, causing them to crash sideways into each other as the ship lurched this way and that. But worse was to happen.

The tank deck was awash with seawater about 2 feet deep. Water poured in from the ramp aperture, as apparently it had not been properly secured (shades of the Newhaven Ferry disaster forty years on). As the tanks and guns collided and rebounded, they crushed many of the Jerrycans full of petrol that had been strapped to the outside of the vehicles. The result was a noxious and dangerous mixture of seawater and petrol giving off choking fumes that made breathing difficult. There was also the risk of fire. Moreover, the effects of the tanks banging into the side of the ship punctured the inner wall protecting cabins, and one could only hope that the outer walls would similarly not be breached.

The Battery Commander (BC), Major Smythe-Osbourne, joined me on the gangway, but we were helpless spectators; there was nothing we could do. No one could venture any further down the gangway, nor get anywhere near the tanks and guns for fear of being crushed. Eventually, the American crew somehow managed to seal the faulty ramp closure and to pump out much of the tainted seawater; attempts were then made to resecure the Sextons. I turned to the Troop for assistance, but half of them were still disposing of their meal in an unnatural way, while the other half wisely found other more urgent things to do. The BC was furious. He was a firebrand, eager to get to grips with the enemy, and for a few moments he saw his aspirations and ambitions about to sink to the bottom of the sea. I climbed back up the gangway with him and heard him muttering mysteriously, 'This will separate the sheep from the goats.'

We spent the nights of 13 and 14 June on board while we rounded the coast and proceeded westwards, but more drama was yet to befall us. At some time in the early morning of the 14th, as our convoy approached the southern coast of the Isle of Wight ('Piccadilly' in naval terms), we turned to port. Shortly afterwards the ship struck some submerged obstacle, causing it to shudder, rear up and assume a list to port. There was a horrible scraping sound from the bottom of the ship and as I apprehensively leaned on the rails to find out what was going on, I saw to my amazement and alarm some of the American crew boarding a lowered lifeboat! Were they abandoning the ship or were they bent on some form of investigation? I'm afraid I thought the worst! The ship limped on for a short distance and then began to go round in circles – something had happened to the steering gear. This was disconcerting because we were part of an enormous convoy and the other ships that filled the horizon had to manoeuvre around us, wondering, no doubt, what on earth we were up to.

It seems that the ship's young American captain, somewhat destabilized by the damage to his craft, and exhausted after several previous trips under fire, became keen to abort the sailing and make it back home, but he hadn't reckoned with our Colonel 'Bob' Daniell. The story goes that there was an altercation between him and the Captain and some spoke of the production of a revolver, as a result of which the ship somehow came mostly under control and resumed its journey towards France, where we beached at about 1500hrs on 15 June (D+9), rather later than our intended time. I did not know we were already two days late!

After all the trials and tribulations of the crossing, the Regiment had a dry landing. As a result of the altercation between the Captain and the Colonel, the ship was pointed directly at the beach and driven there at speed. Although this was apparently the adopted procedure in these unusual circumstances, we did it with some considerable emphasis on the wrong tide! Disembarking was tricky because the ship was literally grounded and the leading edge of the lowered ramp for some reason didn't quite reach beach level. The tanks and guns were nevertheless unloaded rather bumpily, although I think the soft vehicles had to wait a while.

# Chapter 7

# The Run-up to
# Operation Epsom

—⚬—

T he scenes on the beach were almost indescribable. The Beach
Master headed us off a few hundred yards westwards to a
somewhat less busy sector in the sand dunes. To the left of our
beaching point, I could see hundreds of vehicles of all types going hither
and thither, with hordes of men milling around loading and unloading
ships (Mulberry Harbour was still being built). Although the beach area
was free from enemy attention by artillery, there was the sound of gunfire
in the distance, with a few shells bursting about a mile away. The Luftwaffe
with its FW109s also made an unwelcome appearance about this time, and
everything seemed to be firing at them from ships and from land, but they
flew away untouched after dropping a few bombs nearby.

The Regiment disembarked on 15 June at Graye-sur-Mer, which is a
seaside suburb just west of Courseille (Juno Beach), where the 3rd
Canadian Division had landed on D-Day. The Beach Master had directed
us to a basin-shaped area up and behind the dunes where we met our
advance party, disposed of the superfluous waterproof shields, and
prepared the guns for immediate and impending action. (I re-visited this
area in 1998 and found the site almost unchanged.)

Don Troop, and possibly Charlie Troop, set off southwards following
the Troop Leader, Second Lieutenant Charles Coad (who will appear many
times in this narrative). He seemed to know where he was going (or perhaps
he was being led by a guide), but I didn't. I had expected to be hurled into
action right away and a trip through the Normandy countryside was
something of an anti-climax. The first thing I noticed as we drove down
the rural roads was the proliferation of signs erected by the Canadians,
stating baldly that 'Dust Means Death'. Other signs were more ominous,
but helpful, written in German stating 'Minen Verboten', or 'Achtung

Minen', with the minefields nicely fenced off by the Royal Engineers. From not far distant, the gunfire I heard on landing continued unabated, with the occasional shell throwing up plumes of debris a mile or so inland. Huge shells shrieked overhead, fired from Allied warships anchored off the coast, the noise sounding like steam trains passing through a station at speed.

I was interested to see the men's reactions to all this. Only a handful of us had been to France before (we wore the 1939 medal ribbon),[1] but for the others it was clearly something new and exciting, and they viewed it in that context. They took in the beachhead in the manner of tourists on their annual holidays abroad, looking round at unfamiliar sights, and pointing here and there. The danger that might lurk around the next corner did not seem to register.

It might be helpful at this stage to describe briefly the nature of the Normandy countryside over which we were shortly to fight two bloody battles. Apart from the beaches, the immediate countryside consisted mostly of open country of cornfields and meadows. Here and there were orchards and copses. At scattered intervals were small settlements, the profiles of which were broken by the inevitable church spires or towers. Generally, the land sloped gently upwards, and was usually referred to as the Caen-Falaise Plain.

The 'bocage'[2] country lay to the west and south of Caen. It is an extensive area, made up of small, embanked fields and narrow lanes, lined with thick hedgerows. Roughly south of a line Caen-St. Lo is the larger area of undulating country bocage, known as la Suisse Normande.

To return to the narrative, Charles Coad, our Troop Leader at the time, led us cautiously along dusty roads around Courseille, through Banville on to Cully (9176),[3] midway between the Caen-Bayeux road (N13) and the D22. Our journey ended at about 1700 hrs in Cully in uncertain weather that was soon to worsen. The Battery laagered in an orchard belonging to a farm just south of the village (9176) and I wondered what would come next, as we had been told nothing yet of our future tasks.

---

1 My four gun sergeants and myself had served with the British Expeditionary Force in France in 1939, and were expelled through Dunkirk in 1940.
2 '*Bocage*' in French means grove or coppice.
3 The first two numbers are 'eastings' and the second numbers are 'northings'. Map references are normally recorded in three figures of each.

At 0600 hrs the next day (16 May) we were treated to an air battle between six Spitfires and a lone FW109, but he got away. The rest of the day was spent in gun and vehicle maintenance, but on the 17th, at 1720 hrs, a single 88mm shell exploded on our position, wounding Gunner Laven, one of the cooks and now our first casualty. It was probably an enemy gun emptying its barrel at maximum range before moving on; the event was certainly not repeated. On the 18th, a divisional church service was held in a barn nearby, but on the 19th, things began to happen. At 1400 hrs, orders were given to reconnoitre gun positions at a position identified by the map reference 9373, and although we waited anxiously to occupy them, the immediate danger passed and we remained where we were for another day or so.

On the 21st, at 1400 hrs, we occupied other gun positions that had been marked out south of the road north-west of Putot-en-Bessin (8873), and at 2100 hrs, 200 rounds per gun (rpg) were brought in from the dumps. This activity was to support, if necessary, the Canadians who were being attacked by German armour from the 21st SS Panzer Division that appeared to be intent on forcing a passage to the beaches to separate us from the American forces to the west. The Canadians beat off this attack, so we were not called upon to fire. The next day, after spending an uncomfortable night in inclement weather, the officers were told at 1400 hrs of an impending operation, but no details were forthcoming. The 23rd and 24th were spent in consolidating our gun positions, and on the 25th, at 1100 hrs, Brigadier Roscoe Harvey briefed all officers about what was expected of us in the battle to come, code-named Operation Epsom. On the 25th, at 1645 hrs, we at last took up our first operational position (8871), for Operation Epsom. Whilst all this was happening, battles continued elsewhere, with the 43rd (Wessex) Division fighting around Hottot and Tilly nearby.

Before proceeding on to the account of Operation Epsom, it might be helpful to describe a somewhat domestic feature of the composition of 'D' Troop. Don Troop had been formed in late 1940, since when little had changed in its structure. Over that period of nearly four years, each gun subsection or gun team had assumed a family unity of its own, with some indefinable distinctions formed by this intimacy and its sense of identity, which were jealously guarded.

Four of my nine sergeants each commanded a gun subsection, and, like their men, they came from all parts of the country. Sgt Davies ('E' Sub) came from Birmingham; Sgt Musker ('F' Sub) came from Crewe; Sgt Moran ('G' Sub) was from Oxford; and Sgt Barratt ('H' Sub) was from Blandford. Even so, everyone mixed in together within his 'family', and not once in four years was their any serious domestic trouble, except for the usual British soldier's endearing trait of bizarre dark humour that usually took the form of dire (but empty) insults hurled at each other. In my Troop there was the never-ending repartee whereby anyone who did not live in, say, London, Manchester, Liverpool, Cardiff, Newcastle or Glasgow had been deprived of the decencies of a civilized culture.

I was proud of my Troop and of the men within it. Of the gun sergeants, although they all got on very well together, there were distinctions. Davies was a blond, good-looking man, whom we shall meet later. Charlie Musker, our senior sergeant, was a thoughtful man and was well liked. He was to succeed me in due course when I returned to England eight months later. Frank Moran was not given to displaying much emotion, but was a most dependable person. George Barrett was the most interesting person. He was the oldest of us, was grizzled in a macho, handsome way, had an engaging smile and was an inveterate scrounger of useful commodities. I liked them all. Each one was extremely good at his job of commanding a gun subsection and I rated them the best in the Regiment. What they thought about me is open to conjecture!

Looking at the picture overall, the days between the landing and the beginning of operations were most confused, seemingly chaotic, so to complete the events before Operation Epsom, I continued to organize the unceasing task of gun and vehicle maintenance, while elsewhere the plans for the forthcoming battle were being drawn up, although at my level as Troop Sergeant Major I knew nothing of this. The weather was bad, with gusty cold winds and bursts of rain, and it grew steadily worse, culminating in the Great Storm of 19 to 22 June. The artificial harbour known as Mulberry, at the American beach of Omaha at St Laurent, was destroyed and abandoned, while the British section at Arromanches was badly damaged. Even so, by the 22nd, when the storm abated, 600,000 men had been landed, as were 81,000 vehicles of all sorts and 183,000 tons of stores.

During this miserable and very wet period in the run-up to Epsom, because of the peripatetic nature of my duties, I had no time to care for myself, especially in the matter of shelter from the elements, other than what could be improvised from my own equipment and from 'liberated' items. My accommodation at this time was no more than a shallow trench dug in the wet soil, with a groundsheet for overhead cover. The men sheltered in or close to their guns and vehicles, but as Troop BSM I was a 'floater' in this situation, not belonging to any particular vehicle. Jock Forbes, the Battery Sergeant Major, then took pity on me and found dryer accommodation for me in a barn occupied by Battery Headquarters.

The battle that was to start (for us) began on 26 June, eleven days after our landing on the beaches, and although the time spent had been useful, we were keyed up in not knowing what was happening day to day, nor what would happen the next day. But now our war was about to begin.

# Chapter 8

# Operation Epsom

—⁂—

It has been said that in any major campaign there usually has to be a bloodbath, and this is precisely what took place during Operation Epsom (so named because it was planned to take place in Derby week), in which many men and much materiel were lost, for little gain.

Although I knew little, if anything, of what was being planned overall (a nagging theme that will appear from time to time as this narrative progresses), I did learn a little of the composition of the command structure of the day, as it affected us. We apparently belonged to VIII Corps, commanded by Lieutenant General Sir Richard O'Connor of Western Desert fame. The Corps principally consisted of three divisions, two of infantry and one armoured – 15th Scottish, 43rd Wessex, and 11th Armoured (our parent unit). It also had under command the 31st Tank Brigade and the 4th Armoured Brigade. All in all, VIII Corps at this time had 60,000 men and 600 tanks.

The 11th Armoured Division comprised two brigades, 29th Armoured Brigade and 159th Infantry Brigade, the former of which included us – 13th (HAC) Regiment, Royal Horse Artillery, whose prime role was to be supportive of the armour. The 29th Armoured Brigade comprised 3rd Royal Tank Regiment, 2nd Fife and Forfar Yeomanry and the 23rd Hussars, as well as the 8th Rifle Brigade. Of the three 8-gun batteries in 13th RHA, 'G' Battery usually supported the Fife and Forfars, 'H' Battery mostly supported 3rd Tanks and 'I' Battery trailed the 23rd Hussars (although these supportive formations changed from time to time as the Normandy and other campaigns progressed).

Opposing us in the forthcoming battles (as I was to learn later) was, among others, Kurt Meyer's 12th *Hitlerjugend* SS Panzer Division, a fanatical division of young men (or boys) who chose to fight to the death in defence of the Führer's Reich, rather than ignominiously surrender. Recruiting 16,000 volunteers from the Hitler Youth Movement in 1943, the

*Hitlerjugend* comprised fanatical seventeen to nineteen year olds inculcated by Nazi ideology. We had to face them in the upcoming battle, and we had a taste of their will to fight to the death.

In addition to the *Hitlerjugend*, the elite Panzer Lehr were immediately out in front of us, together with the 21st SS Panzer Division. They held 10 miles of the front, along which offensive action was continuous. Behind these formations was *SS-Obersturmbannfuhrer* Mohnke's 12th SS Panzer Regiment. In all, these units had fifty-eight operational Panzer Mk IVs and forty-four Panzer Mk V (Panther) tanks, backed by the guns of 12th SS Artillery Regiment, and seventeen heavy anti-tank guns. Deployed north of the River Odon were four companies of dual-purpose 88mm guns belonging to 4th *FlakSturmregiment*, with an uncommitted reserve of half-tracks and armoured cars. 1st *SS Panzercorps*, comprising two tank companies of 56-ton Panzer VI (Tiger) tanks, were on the move up to the front.

Operation Epsom was VIII Corps' first battle in Europe and General Montgomery had promised General Eisenhower a lightning breakthrough. His amended battle plan of 23 June (which had been postponed for two days due to the bad weather) stated that VIII Corps would deliver the main attack. 'VIII Corps will be switched to form part of the right, or western wing of the pincer movement. The final objective will remain [Bretteville-sur-Laize], but the Corps will advance to this objective on the general thrust line ST MAUVIEU[1] 9269 – ESQUAY 9460 – AMAYE-SUR-ODON 9757.' Thus, Phase One was the crossing of the Odon, and the second phase was the crossing of the Orne River (the Objective of the Plan). The Great Storm caused a postponement of forty-eight hours, and VIII Corps was tasked to begin the Epsom battle on 26 June, although 49th Division began their attack at 0400 hrs on the 25th, fighting for Vendes (south of Fontenay) and the larger village of Fontenay. I knew none of these plans at troop level and identify them now from reading detailed histories of the battle.

The plans of VIII Corps were flexible, as it was not known what to expect, but the 15th Scottish Division was ordered to attack at 0730 hrs on Monday, 26 June to secure crossings over the Odon River between Gavrus and Verson. The first objective would be the villages of St Mauvieu and Cheux, and the second objective was the crossing of the River Odon.

11th Armoured Division was positioned to exploit any successes of 15th

---

1 Some historians call this Manvieu.

Scottish, and be ready to pass its tanks through the river bridgeheads at a moment's notice; it was in the latter Phase Two that we saw action. This involved 29th Armoured Brigade being ordered to capture Hill 112, passing through St Mauvieu and Cheux after their capture by the 44th Lowland Brigade of the 15th Scottish Division. We moved to our Forming-up Position (8871) at 1645 hrs on the 25th, listening to the distant skirl of the pipes of the Scotsmen.

Sunday the 25th was cold, wet, gloomy and miserable. We had no rainproof clothing and although the wearing of a waterproof gas cape, which was normally rolled up on our backs, would have kept us fairly dry, its use for that purpose was strictly forbidden (we still had the notion that the enemy might use gas). We either suffered in a wet battle dress, or wore an overcoat, although the latter was not really an option because it was difficult, hot and sweaty to operate guns when encumbered by a heavy wet coat.

The combination of eleven days of mostly enforced inaction between landing and Epsom, spent in dreadful weather, had sobered up my spirits considerably, but the knowledge that I was now about to begin my particular war was a welcoming feature. All officers were given their final briefing on the artillery plan at 1100 hrs on the 25th. We were to fire a barrage, along with 700 other guns, in support of the 15th Scottish Division. At 1645 hrs, therefore, 'H' Battery, of which Don Troop formed part, moved in driving rain to its Forming-up Position north of the Caen-Caumont road (D9) in the vicinity of Putot-en-Bessin (8871). This, our first gun position, was a small field bounded by hedges and stubby trees, with guns spaced about 25 yards apart. I spent this sullen and sodden night trudging from gun to gun checking on crews, ammunition and food (although the latter had low priority due to battle conditions), posting sentries and making sure everyone knew what they had to do.

This night of 25/26 June was spent in pouring rain in a mood of apprehension, not modified by the miserable environment. No one slept. The gun command post staff, including myself, worked feverishly under dim lights to compute the barrage data required to be put on the guns that were to fire over a 4-mile front. The direction of fire had to be calculated and the ranges accurately determined. In addition, data had to be construed in respect of angles of sight and type of charge being used to propel the shell up the barrel. Meteorological conditions were reduced to numbers and circulated in a Meteorological Telegram, and corrections to the gun data made accordingly. Separate data for the individual guns were calculated (as no two guns fire identically). Most important was the setting of the 'lift' lines. This meant that the guns fired at one range 50 or so yards in front of the advancing infantry, and, at selected times, depending (hopefully) on the rate of advance, the range was increased by a further incremental 50 yards with the infantry following up behind, and so on, until this incremental firing reached its stop line. It was a delicate operation requiring great accuracy, otherwise shells would fall on the attacking infantry (not an unknown experience, and known as 'friendly fire'). The barrage was originally timed to begin at 0645 hrs on Monday, 26 June, but was put back to 0730 hrs (we were not told why). Part of my job was to ensure that the gun sergeants knew exactly what they had to do and this meant trailing from gun to gun in the dark, cold and wet night, with no thought of sleep.

As the time for the opening barrage came nearer, apprehension turned to mounting excitement. Some distance behind us, about 700 guns (300 from VIII Corps and 400 from 3rd Canadian) fired to begin the main battle, aided by monitors and cruisers of the Royal Navy firing their 12-inch and 15inch heavy guns offshore. Our role was different. Our 25-pdrs, mounted on Sextons, were in support of 3rd Royal Tank Regiment. Whenever they moved forward, so did we. We were mobile, whilst the supporting towed guns to the rear were more or less stationary for longer periods.

The noise from this barrage of guns was ear-splitting, with shells of all sizes screaming over our heads, crashing not very far in front of us and exploding in flames, smoke and debris. The thick ground mist that enveloped the battlefield held the fumes in an acrid fog, causing runny eyes, noses and choking throats. The bonus was that in this first position the enemy did not direct their guns in our direction, although plenty of lethal activity was going on to our immediate front as the Scotsmen began their attack.

The gun sergeants had made bets as to which gun would fire the first round to mark Don Troop's first positive entry into the war. The GPO in charge of the Troop's Command Post (then Lieutenant Harold Fost) nervously glued his eyes to his watch, ticking off the minutes and seconds from 0715 hrs onwards. My immediate job was to stand behind the guns with a compass in case anything should go wrong (not an unknown experience, as shouted orders can be misinterpreted in battle conditions). The GPO issued warning noises during the countdown, his voice rising in a manner that would have done justice to a horse-racing commentator.

The Scotsmen were to attack the small village of Mercelet (945685), located between Carpiquet (960690) and Cheux (910670). This village was also our first target, which was held tenaciously by the *Hitlerjugend*. The GPO gave the countdown: 'GET READY. SIX, FIVE, FOUR, THREE, TWO, ONE, FIRE.²' On the precise stroke of 0730 hrs, the four guns, with the other twenty of the regiment, opened up, firing their first rounds in anger – and that's where the cheating began! My gun sergeants laid bets on who would get off the first round. Sgt Davies of 'E' sub argued that he was the first to fire, but he was held to have cheated because he shot fractionally between 'ONE' and 'FIRE', so he had some difficulty in collecting his bets! This controversy extended widely with 'I' Battery claiming that they fired the first shots of the Regiment. The matter was never resolved, although it happily rumbled on for weeks to come. Such are the horrors of war!

Our initial contribution to the required destruction of the enemy lasted half an hour, during which time, the noise was indescribable. Our 25-pdrs were firing 'rapid fire' which meant that rounds were fired as fast as they could be loaded, and when they did fire, the report was like a heavy blow in the face and ears. At the same time, shells of all sizes screamed overhead and explosions merged into one continuous crashing roar, inter-mingled with the sharp crackle of machine-gun fire. Together with billowing smoke and fumes, imprisoned by the heavy ground mist, this cacophony produced a stupefying orchestra of noise and physical discomfort that most of the men had not experienced before. And that was only the Allied side! The Germans retaliated in front of us, with a countering fire of shells and mortars falling on the brave Scotsmen. It was like Dante's Inferno in sound and vision.

Shortly afterwards, at 0834 hrs, we joined in with others to produce another artillery concentration of fire. The target was a group of farmhouses south of Mercelet (935676), south-east of St Mauvieu and east of Cheux, where enemy infantry (1/26 SS Panzer Grenadier Regiment), and possibly tanks, were forming up. We continued firing for a while, taking some prisoners, then at 1100 hrs moved into our second position of the day at about a kilometre south-west of Norrey-en-Bessin in the valley of the River Mue (9169). This move, occasioned by the forward probing of 3rd

---

2  The GPO started at 'SIX' because 'FIVE' can be mistaken for 'FIRE' in the midst of a cacopheny of noise.

Royal Tanks in the wake of the grim advance of the 44th Lowland Infantry Brigade, was not without incident.

By 1230 hrs 3 RTR was in the area south of Norrey-en-Bessin, ready to make a dash for the River Odon. We moved south-east through the high-standing corn at a snail's pace, moving from Putot-en-Bessin, nose to tail, following behind the tanks, and crossing over the Start Line from whence the battle began. The tension among the gun crews increased because the move took us from the reasonably safe position behind the frontal attack of the 15th Scottish Division into the midst of what we now expected to be a tank battle in which we would play our part. On the outskirts of Norrey-en-Bessin we joined a track leading southwards with the village of Norrey to our left and a large open cornfield to our right, thus making a crossing over the D179. The topography of the ground was such that there was a barely noticeable gentle slope down to the small stream of the Mue, but before reaching it we were momentarily in view of the enemy on our left (12th SS *Hitlerjugend*) who were holding out at Carpiquet airfield where the forward observers of the German 12th SS Artillery Regiment were strongly entrenched. They had previously been firing indirectly at targets just behind the British barrage, but now with us in view they had something more direct to shoot at!

Lining this lane on our left was a small hedge that we hugged wherever possible, but it was not continuous, so for the first time we came under enemy observed fire (our baptism, as it were). The shells from their 88mm anti-aircraft guns and other artillery pieces, aimed at our leading tanks, shrieked uncomfortably low overhead, exploding with a great deal of noise in the cornfield immediately on our right, throwing up mounds of earth and stones, and scattering hot steel shell splinters, together with uncomfortable pressure waves caused by the blasts. The tankers in front simply battened down and proceeded slowly on their way, but we had no such complete shelter in our Sextons. The armoured sides of our guns were only waist high so one had to crouch down on one's knees to escape lethal splinters coming in parallel to the ground, but we could not escape shrapnel from above, so we were covered in muck and dust and enveloped in acrid smoke. Fortunately the billowing smoke made their aim somewhat erratic and we were lucky not to be hit. That cannot be said of the Scottish infantrymen nearby who were suffering very heavy casualties. The battlefield was becoming more ominous as shells and mortars exploded all around, and we passed burning and exploding tanks that had been hit by enemy fire, with blackened survivors struggling to find shelter. The noise was cacophonic and one did not know where or how to take cover.

The weather continued to be wet, dark and gloomy, with the thick ground mist slowly clearing, but being replaced by dense patches of smoke from the artillery barrage and burning vehicles. The Scotsmen were having a rough time of it, suffering casualties all round. The 6th Royal Scots Fusiliers crossed the River Mue, closely following behind the artillery barrage, and advancing towards and through the outposts of the Hitlerjugend to St Mauvieu which was strongly held by the 12th SS Engineer Battalion and the 1/26 Panzer Grenadier Regiment. The enemy had converted St Mauvieu's stone buildings into a strongly fortified position and caused many losses to the Scotsmen from artillery fire, diminishing their capacity for fighting (on the 26th alone, the 15th Scottish Division had 2,720 young men killed, wounded or missing).

We came into action at a point inside the shallow valley just north of the Mue between les Saullets and St Mauvieu. It was by no means a peaceful occupation and among many other activities we captured four very sullen boys from the Hitlerjugend. The noise from all arms was ear-splitting, and enemy shell and mortar fire came uncomfortably close (it was to get much worse). At 1500 hrs, with our tanks advancing on Gavrus and Tourmauville, we began firing on a line of about 190 degrees at targets in the villages of Rauray and La Haut du Bosq (9066), south-west of Cheux (9167), as part of a regimental concentration of twenty-four guns, firing 350 rounds per gun (rpg). This was heavy shooting indeed and my four guns alone put down about 20 tons of high explosive on enemy positions. We were not, however, immune from their retaliation and our firing was interrupted by very heavy enemy fire coming onto the gun position. We had to take cover from time to time, but the firing programme had to continue, and fortunately we had no casualties.

The enemy, especially the fanatical *Hitlerjugend*, sheltered in the waist-high corn, supported by positions dug in in the surrounding orchards, hedgerows and farm buildings. The *Jugend*, fighting like demons, infested the battlefield and caused many hold-ups. Don Troop found itself in the midst of it all when the enemy shelling and mortaring became more intense. At 1500 hrs, we fired into La Haut du Bosq (9066), expending seventy rounds per gun. Our immediate opponents were the 8th Werfer (Mortar) Brigade armed with *Nebelwerfers*, which are six-barrelled weapons, each barrel firing a 150mm (or 220cm) bomb fitted with a siren that screamed obscenely as it descended. The noise is terrifying and it did much to affect the morale of the men on the receiving end, quite apart from the lethal effects of the exploding metal. We called these mortars 'Moaning Minnies'. We were lucky in that the mortars just missed our gun position by a matter of yards.

We were fighting for our lives at this period in the battle and we stayed in this dangerous position through the night of the 26th. Targets came in thick and fast, and there were hardly any pauses between firing at one and taking on another; there was no time for relaxation of any kind. If the occasional pause did come along, the gunners spent it mainly clearing away spent shell cases, and sorting and restocking ammunition, tasks that were my direct responsibility. The gun position still continued to be heavily shelled, which made my job extremely unpleasant as I had to move in the open from gun to gun. The whole scenario was barely describable, with guns blasting off, shells and mortar bombs exploding among us, and smoke and cordite fumes polluting the damp air. The noise was deafening and made communication between us almost impossible.

At 0700 hrs the next day, the 27th, we were continuously in action supporting the tanks of 29th Armoured Brigade, and this went on without a break as the hours passed. The 3rd Royal Tanks were fighting in the area east of La Haut du Bosq (9366) and, in their support, we fired 120 rounds per gun. We stayed the night in this most unpleasant position and midnight saw us firing continuously in support of the armour, going on until midday on the 28th, when we did some shooting on targets in the area south of Gavrus (9261). At 1200 hrs we moved to a position near Cheux (915610) where we were immediately stonked, which gave us little expectation of an easier existence.

At the gun position I had little idea what we were shooting at as we simply responded to the seemingly chaotic fire orders ceaselessly coming down over the wireless net. The Forward Observation Officers up with the tanks rarely bothered, or had time, to say what the targets were – they were too busy observing, acquiring and eliminating them. One of my jobs during this Dante-like scenario was to see that the guns wanted for nothing, whether firing or not, especially in the matter of ammunition stocks and fuel. I was thus continuously on the move, flitting from gun to gun, trying to shout above the cacophony of noise and keeping my head down when things got a little too uncomfortable. In retrospect, it was a dangerous task because, as a lone figure scurrying from gun to gun, totally

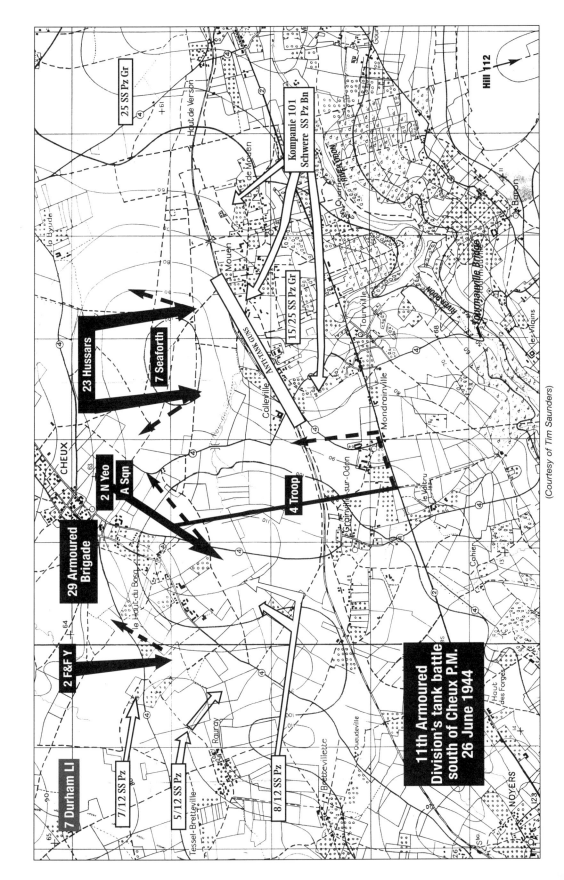

(Courtesy of Tim Saunders)

Hill 112

25 SS Pz Gr

Kompanie 101
Schwere SS Pz Bn

QUARRY

TAVERBON

Baron

RIVER ODON

15/25 SS Pz Gr

de Mouen

Mouen

Tourville

Colleville

Mondrainville

Tourmauville Bridge

23 Hussars

7 Seaforth

CHEUX

2 N Yeo
A Sqn

4 Troop

Grainville-sur-Odon

le Valtru

Cahier

ANTI-TANK GUN

29 Armoured
Brigade

le Haut-du-Bosq

2 F & Y

7 Durham LI

Rauray

7/12 SS Pz

5/12 SS Pz

8/12 SS Pz

Tessel-Bretteville

Bretteville

Queudeville

Haut
des Forges

NOYERS

11th Armoured
Division's tank battle
south of Cheux P.M.
26 June 1944

exposed to either a direct hit or from shrapnel, the chances of getting away with it were somewhat remote. But Providence was kind!

Each gun was firing series of 'Five Rounds Gunfire' almost without pause, which meant that as one round went off, the gun was immediately reloaded and fired. Because the gun barrels had only four degrees of traverse either way, any directions outside those limits meant that the whole gun chassis had to be moved by the driver engaging gears, revving the engine and shunting this way and that, so the engines continuously had to be kept going more or less at half throttle, adding to the indescribable burden on the ears and increasing the tension of the gunners. Enemy shelling continued to plaster the gun position, and it was a miracle that we suffered no casualties, although deafness and fatigue played a part. There was no time to feel hungry, or if one did feel its pangs there was no immediate way of appeasing them.

The gun position was sited at the bottom of the shallow valley just behind the Mue stream, with the ground rising gently behind us, and, because of this configuration, some enemy shells and mortars landed about a hundred yards to the rear of the guns, although this did not save us from the piercing showers of red hot slivers of metal and earth debris that peppered the armoured sides of the guns. Yet it was in this situation that I had to run from gun to gun in response to garbled demands from the gun sergeants, keep check, among other tasks, on the ammunition stocks remaining and arrange for more supplies to come up from the rear echelon where the back-up reserves were kept.

During one of these many occasions I had the idea of taking my Bren carrier to a place immediately behind the guns, about a hundred yards away, where the recent shelling had taken place, as we had been warned that we might be attacked from the Cristot area on the right flank, or even from the rear, such was the fluidity of the situation. I thought this action on my part to be prudent – the carrier was armed with a heavy 0.50 Browning machine gun and would create a nuisance among any Germans who ventured within range. I took with me Driver Smith and Lance Bombardier Muscoe. Unfortunately the Germans decided to intensify their mortaring, lifting their range so that mortar bombs fell thick and fast in the hundred yards or so between the guns and us, isolating us from the meagre shelter of the guns. We had no shelter other than the vulnerable carrier, so in the midst of this mortaring we just had to claw the ground in the open and hope for the best, although the others preferred to shelter underneath the carrier. The noise was terrific and frightening, but we had no alternative but to stick it out. Although badly shaken, by some miracle the shrapnel and earth debris propelled by the exploding mortar bombs mostly passed over us, so we only caught the blast, pressure waves, heat and the acrid smoke. We escaped injury other than temporary shock, but the blasts tore our clothing. We returned to the guns when the stonking died down, looking like smoke-blackened tramps. I was not very popular with my small crew!

In this context of extreme danger, the effects of being under shell and mortar fire are difficult to describe, for at the time one's normal emotions are in suspense. To be lucky, one has to be able to hear the approach of the missile. Failure to hear it usually means that it is too late. A shell comes in with a swishing noise, like a fast passing train, until it hits the ground – or its target. On impact the noise is numbing, with a crack that hits the ears like a whiplash and can cause painful deafness. The explosion of a shell (if one is unfortunate to be so close as to observe it) produces a vicious red and white flash, followed immediately by debris propelled at speed, both vertically and laterally, comprised of earth and steel fragments (sometimes called shrapnel) that can have a lethal range of up to a hundred yards radius (depending on the weight and size of the missile). The blast also causes pressure waves that can easily kill a man, or knock him over. All this lethal activity, happening at once, produces choking smoke from burning cordite. If one is unlucky enough to be hit by a shell fragment, the metal will be red hot and cauterizes the flesh as well as tearing it. It was in these circumstances that I clawed the ground for non-existent shelter as the mortar bombs burst all around us, although we were fortunate to escape, shocked, but more or less unharmed.

After this exciting affair, the shelling and mortaring eased off; I looked around this most unhealthy gun position, and could just see the battered church of Norrey-en-Bessin behind me, and in front the damaged church of St Mauvieu. The ground occupied by the Troop had only a few hours earlier been the killing ground of the Scotsmen who had fought their way forward in the face of bitter opposition from the fanatical *Hitlerjugend*, and the evidence was there to see. The field was heavily cratered and littered with possibly a hundred or more dead bodies obscenely huddled in grotesque shapes, both Scotsmen and Germans alike. It was an awful sight. Some bodies were torn to pieces, yet some seemed untouched, killed simply by blast. The air was thick with smoke and acrid cordite fumes, and the smell of death. It was a sobering thought to know that perhaps only an hour ago these were living, able-bodied young men! During such slight pauses as there were, I suggested rather diffidently to some of the chaps on the guns that they might try to bury some of our dead, or at least cover them up, but the men were too shocked by the sight to comply, and were glad when firing was resumed, when they could became otherwise engaged.

The fanaticism of the young men/boys of the 12th *Hitlerjugend* Division, who were aged around eighteen (although some seemed to be younger), arising from blind, indoctrinated minds, was difficult to comprehend. I can recount an example of this.

As already described, the gun position occupied the reverse slope leading down to the River Mue, which meant that the Germans had been facing uphill as the Scotsmen came downhill, slight gradient though it was. A few yards from my Bren carrier lay a dead German, sprawled face downward, his hands outstretched above his head, facing the advancing Scots. He had been shot in the back. Gingerly, I turned him over to find his identity papers and was surprised to see that he was older than I expected him to be, probably in his mid-thirties. Certainly, he was not a Hitler Youth. Twenty yards or so behind him was another dead German who was unmistakeably a Hitler Youth from the 12th SS *Hitlerjugend* Division. His papers showed that he was barely eighteen years old. He was still grasping his weapon that was pointing directly at the dead man in front. The evidence seemed to indicate that the older man might have been in the act of surrendering to the Scotsmen and the youth behind had shot him in the back. This dastardly act may have been seen by a Scotsman, for the boy was shot cleanly between the eyes, probably immediately after his murderous act.

For some reason, probably to take reverse compass readings because of the shelling and mortaring still going on immediately to our rear, I had to go forward of the guns on foot over this graveyard for about a hundred yards to the bank of the shallow Mue stream that was lined with small scattered trees and bushes. I had to do this because although I would normally stand behind the guns to take readings, the ground to the rear was still being chewed up by enemy shellfire. As I approached the little grouping of trees by the banks of the stream, a Glaswegian apparition roughly accosted me and enquired of my presence there in some barely comprehensible dialect (these were not quite his exact words!). He was swiping a bloodstained bayonet, as were a few other men with him. These were part of the remnants of the Scottish regiment that had taken heavy casualties and this small group was determined to go forward again in the teeth of the enemy only a short distance away. Suddenly, I felt very small in the presence of such men and was glad I was not an infantryman.

This, the opening day, Tuesday, 26 June, of Operation Epsom was an eventful day for us in our first taste of battle, suffering casualties, but it had been a frustrating day for the tanks of the 11th Armoured Division. The River Odon objective had not been reached, although some units of 29th Armoured Brigade held a small bridgehead across the river, and the enemy still occupied the high ground to the west. It had been raining on and off all day, but in the evening the rain came down in torrents, continuing on into the 27th. The water table of the Mue valley, never far from the surface at this point, rose, and the ground became waterlogged. Movement was therefore difficult for the Sextons, compounded by their constant changes in the direction of fire, resulting in partially digging themselves into the mud. This mud quickly transferred itself to one's person; plastering already wet clothes, which added to the discomfort of the men.

Earlier, at around 1500 hrs, the gallant Scotsmen had taken St Mauvieu, La Haut du Bosq and Cheux, mostly in hand-to-hand fighting, at heavy cost, but the enemy were still all around us. We had fired without pause into the area around La Haut du Bosq, and into Cheux to the south of us, and now the latter area was under very heavy enemy shellfire from German guns as a tank bottleneck built up. The village of Cheux, now converted to rubble, formed a major road junction in this rural locality and the Germans knew it very well, shelling it accordingly. The 9th Royal Tank Regiment lost thirteen of its eighteen tanks in a very short time. In addition, many Germans still milled around in the wet corn and snipers were shooting at tank commanders in particular who, of necessity, had to have head and shoulders above the tank turrets to be aware of what was happening around them.

The 23rd Hussars ran out of ammunition and were pulled back from their probing towards Hill 112, north-east of Esquay, for refuelling and rearming, but we ('H' Battery) stayed in action throughout this very wet night, 26th/27th, firing heavily and continuously on targets as they were acquired. Part of these actions was called Harassing Fire – so named to keep the enemy from relaxing or reforming. This was very tiring for all of us because the opportunities for rest and some sleep were largely denied.

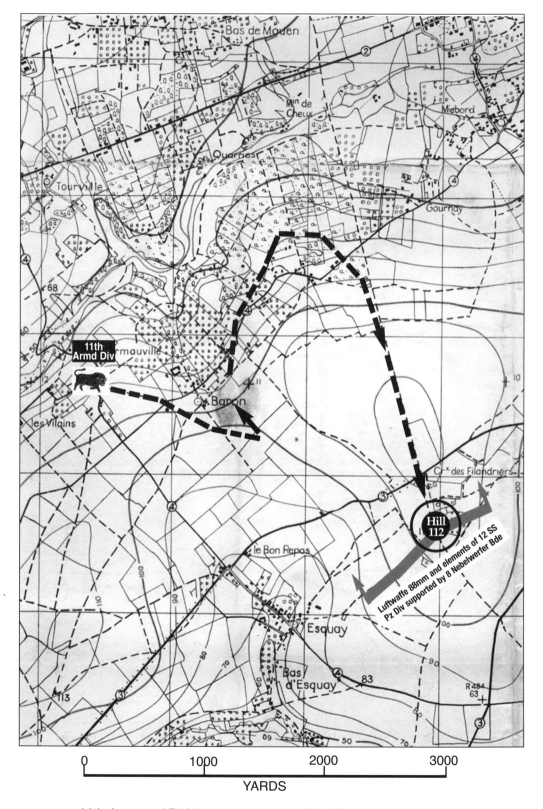

11th Armoured Division's advance on Hill 112. *(Courtesy of Tim Saunders)*

In addition to answering calls for shoots, this was also the time for me to render returns, indent for supplies, construct situation reports, bring the gun history sheets up to date, make good any deficiencies if possible, try to get some food, and a whole host of routine tasks, many of which were in my domain. Sleep was out of the question.

At 1800 hrs, 15th Scottish were ordered to continue the advance on Grainville-sur-Odon and Colleville, with 3 RTR and ourselves in support, reaching Colleville by 2100 hrs. It was by no means quiet, as we came under vicious counter-attacks from the east. That ended the first day of Operation Epsom, having secured a small bridgehead over the River Odon at Tourmauville. We laagered for the night in pouring rain north of Cheux, although sleep and rest were at a premium as gun and vehicle maintenance had to be undertaken, come what may, and ammunition stocks replaced. We also experienced harassing fire from the enemy. The miserable dawn of the 27th did not ease matters.

On the second day of Epsom, we continued firing heavily from 0700 hrs onwards in support of two squadrons of the 23rd Hussars and a company of 8th Rifle Brigade as they fought their way once again in the direction of Hill 112. It was a filthy, wet morning, with drenching rain adding to the chaos of a battlefield. The gun position was almost awash, but within two or three hours we managed to fire 120 rounds per gun. At about 1500 hrs I heard that our sister Troop's ('C' for Charlie) forward observation tank had taken casualties (Gunners Sisk, Wells and Doull), hit by a shell from an enemy Mk IV tank, which also hit a Bren carrier. As my mode of conveyance was a Bren carrier, my doubts as to its vulnerability were confirmed.

The action on both sides became hectic and my Troop alone fired 480 shells, mostly under retaliatory fire. The Germans were not very far from us. Our role as mobile tracked artillery meant that we had to go where the tanks went and the tanks' role, among others, was to occupy enemy territory and to diminish the opposition, so we were mostly always in the thick of the battle. So it was that we were warned of the likely approach of enemy tanks. Shells were beginning to fall upon us from our right as well as from the front and we felt considerably exposed. Our job was to support our tanker friends who were trying to occupy the notorious Hill 112, which meant that we had to ignore the danger of being attacked and to keep on firing willy-nilly.

The intensity of this part of the battle meant that our ammunition expenditure was running at about 150 rounds or more per gun and the effort of doing so under extreme enemy pressure in inclement weather was beginning to take its toll on the performance of the gunners. We had been continuously in action since the evening of the 25th, with little or no sleep for anyone, and it was now midday on the 27th – roughly forty-eight hours of constant effort in dangerous circumstances, moving from one place to another; but there was to be no let-up.

The Troop fired all through the foggy wet night of 27/28 June from midnight to midday, with the tanks moving off at 0500 hrs in the direction of the Odon to support the 15th Scottish and the 43rd Wessex Divisions. We continued firing to about midday on the third day of Epsom, mostly at targets in the area of Gavrus (9261) where the projected crossing of the Odon had failed.

At 1200 hrs on the 28th, in pouring rain, after bearing the brunt of a lively pasting from enemy artillery that shocked us somewhat, we thankfully left Norrey-en-Bessin, which we had christened 'Stonk Alley' because of the immediate intensity of mortar and shellfire falling about us. Our new position, close to Pointe 100 south-east of le Haut-du-Bosq (915660) looking towards Colleville, was, however, just as uncomfortable. The 25th Panzer Grenadier Regiment had recently occupied it and they knew the ground well. As a result, we were immediately and accurately fired upon by heavy mortar fire that kept our heads down, but luckily we suffered no casualties except the usual shock and fear of being hit.

In a very short time the village of Cheux had been almost completely destroyed and the inhabitants had fled, leaving much of their cattle behind. The cows remaining alive were a pitiful sight, unmilked with swollen udders, and in pain with what I was told was milk fever. Fortunately there were not many of these live beasts because most of the stock had been killed by enemy fire (and possibly by our own). The carcasses of the animals that were left were bloated, internal gasses causing them to explode, producing a most nauseating smell. It was so noxious and so sickening that we felt we were better off back in Stonk Alley with all the danger it entailed.

This polluted atmosphere was most noticeable at the Gun Command Post, which was closely sited to one of these carcasses. The configuration of the gun position made the choice of this site inevitable, so I had no alternative but to take steps to remove or eliminate the decaying animal. Drag ropes were attached to it, and attempts made to tow it away using my

Bren carrier, but the deterioration of the flesh merely meant that the carcass came apart. I then tried dousing it with petrol and set fire to it, but the beast refused to burn. The smell was indescribable and some of the men were actually sick. At the same time, the Germans were still pestering us with mortars, so all in all, the memory of Cheux is not one of great affection.

At the same time, around midday, the expected enemy tanks came very close to us, and we received the dreaded warning 'Tank Alert'. The Panzers came almost up to us from the right (west), but fortunately our own armour engaged them and drove them off, but it was a close shave. Sextons were not built to be particularly useful when confronted in a sitting position by a 40-ton monster with a revolving turret and a lethal gun. We kept up the shooting all day right up to midnight, the targets being in the vicinity of Hill 112. We were supporting the 3rd Royal Tanks in their attempts to capture the hill, which was bitterly contested by the Germans, and in the early evening we had to fire red smoke shells to guide in the marauding Typhoons, circling above in the 'cab rank', onto suitable targets. We also fired high-explosive shells into the target and were told (a rare occasion) that between us we managed to destroy at least six Panther Mk V tanks. We followed it up by joining in a regimental shoot of twenty-four guns onto a wood from which more Panthers were 'fished out', and Hill 112 was again momentarily ours. But the German resistance was so strong that 29th Armoured Brigade was ordered to withdraw into Cheux, which they did with much reluctance, despite their casualties.

During this time our Forward Observation Officer (and Troop Commander), Captain Kinnersley, had reached the fearsome Hill 112 in his Sherman tank, alongside the tank squadron he was supporting, but he was wounded by mortar fire, as was Lance Bombardier Darragon, and the tank lost a track. He and his remaining crew tried to effect repairs to the tank, but another mortar bomb landed close by and Gunner Clay, the tank driver, was wounded, as was Captain Kinnersley for the second time; he was eventually evacuated to England. For his courage in getting so far in support of the tankers in hellish circumstances, and at one point giving his own map reference location as a target, he was awarded a Military Cross.

By nightfall on the 28th, 3 RTR reached Hill 112, supported by our fire as midnight passed. We continued firing incessantly at about 150 rpg, from 0001 hrs to 0600 hrs on this the third day of Epsom. Our firing was to cover the lengthy withdrawal to Cheux of 29th Armoured Brigade, which was running short of ammunition and fuel.

We stopped firing at 0630 hrs, as we were ordered back to 'Stonk Alley' at Norrey-en-Bessin (913707), from whence the battle had receded. As the battle had moved on, we were able to indulge for a short while in much-needed gun and vehicle maintenance. 11th Armoured Division had its share (100 tanks and 1,000 casualties) of the 4,020 men lost in VIII Corps in the Epsom battle. Epsom failed in its objectives and there was no breakthrough, but it had created a bulge 6 miles long and 3 miles wide.

# Chapter 9

# Continuing Action

—∿∿—

T hursday, 29 June, marked the formal ending of Operation Epsom, although I was not immediately aware of that happy event (nor were the Germans, apparently!), because we had to stay in action for another nine days or so, firing continuously day and night, supporting all and sundry, it seemed, who needed our services. The armoured elements of the Division had been pulled back to prepare for the next affray, leaving us seemingly available to any formation. I remember that the action during this time was fast and furious, firing day and night. Already we had been in direct contact with the enemy for five days and nights from 25 to 29 June, firing thousands of 25-pdr shells, with the briefest of opportunities for rest and maintenance, but whereas now many units were rested, we remained on the battlefield. We had few fatal casualties during that time (more came later), but others were wounded and were evacuated. Richard Doherty writes:[1] 'As the fourth day of Epsom faded into darkness, Second Army had much cause to be grateful to the Gunners whose skill had been so vital in breaking up German attacks.' We were to stay in action for another seventeen days.

During that time we could be forgiven for feeling a shade confused. We now seemed to be parted from our parent 11th Armoured Division, coming under intermittent command of I, VIII, XII and XXX Corps in battles fought in other sectors (Operations Windsor, Charnwood and Jupiter). On the 29th, therefore, we were sent, at 0630 hrs, to a position close to Norrey-en-Bessin (913707), and stayed there for a few hours until 2200 hrs for much-needed maintenance. We then moved to a position north-west of St Mauvieu in support of the 15th Scottish Division, and fired 30 rounds per gun continuously for two hours, breaking up a Panzer counter-attack on the west flank.

---

1 Doherty, Richard, *Normandy 1944. The Road to Victory*, Spellmount Ltd, 2004, p. 183.

On the 30th, a certain amount of Battery reorganization was carried out, marking the beginning of my new roles. Immediately after Epsom, General Dempsey had turned his attention to the front south of the Odon, which was reinforced by the 43rd (Wessex) Division, whilst our 159th Infantry Brigade came under command of 15th Scottish Division. 11th Armoured, including ourselves, were withdrawn from the advanced positions near Baron and Hill 112. 29th Armoured Brigade was disappointed that it had to abandon Hill 112, for which it had fought so hard. We now faced the 9th SS Panzer Division coming in from Villers Bocage on our west flank. Our targets were west of St Mauvieu (at 918694). We fired for two hours before midnight with an expenditure of 30 rpg on Defensive Fire tasks (or DFs, meaning pre-prepared shoots selected to be fired in the case of any emergencies) on targets usually only a short distance from us. Sometimes we were so far in front that some of the plotted DF targets were actually behind us. It was sometimes the case that we were so far advanced, and so close to the enemy, that our gun positions became targets for someone else.

The next day, 30 June, as already noted, due to casualties and inter-postings, the Troop and Battery command staffs were reorganized, as a result of which I formally became Acting Troop Leader, Relief Gun Position Officer and occasional Forward Observation Officer, while still retaining the duties and rank of Battery Sergeant Major. This was a four-job arrangement that lasted a full eight months almost without interruption.

At 1300 hrs, German 105mm guns and *Nebelwerfers* again shelled and mortared us, but we did not incur any casualties other than the usual discomfort of flying debris, metal splinters and cordite smoke. At 1745 hrs the next day the shelling became intense, making life most uncomfortable, and at 1815 hrs, a regimental concentration was put down on targets at Baron (942622), my Troop alone firing a total of 371 rounds. At 1830 hrs, I watched a hundred Allied bombers dropping their lethal loads on Villers Bocage to discourage the 9th SS from taking any further part in the war – this wasn't entirely successful as we came up against them several times later on. The day's activities ended at 2350 hrs when we drove off another local attack.

The next day, 2 July, was not markedly different from the previous day. Most of the morning we were kept low by the usual intermittent shelling from the troublesome 105s, and this went on until 1750 hrs when the Battery Commander forsook us in favour of shooting the 77th Medium Regiment onto a number of targets, that Regiment being armed with the heavier 5.5-inch guns.

At 0120 hrs on the 3rd, I was the Acting GPO and was kept very busy, firing three times on similar tasks, which meant that the enemy were attacking very close by (we were almost firing over open sights). This firing continued through the night and into the morning, when, at 1145 hrs, eight guns comprising 'Charlie' and 'Don' Troops together fired 798 shells, at a rate of 100 rpg, being the equivalent of each gun depositing a ton of high explosive on the opposition. The Germans were not annihilated, however, as they immediately began shelling us in retaliation. We had five casualties among our supporting Bofors light anti-aircraft guns, proving that we were not immune to such matters; it was just that our luck ran out at last.

Later in the day, at 1805 hrs, after sustaining a further heavy bout of enemy shelling someone had the sense to move us back about 700 yards to a less exposed position on a plateau south of the main road near Putot-en-Bessin (913711), almost back on the Start Line which we had previously occupied what seemed like ages before. We were still engaged in firing DF tasks and stayed a short while in this position until 1130 hrs the following day when a reconnaissance party left to establish a new position south at Mouen (9365), over halfway between the Start Line and the Objective at Hill 112, close to the northern bank of the Odon. Open country gave way to a more enclosed and populated landscape and it proved to be a most unpleasant place, as we found out when the guns moved in at 1500 hrs. For some unexplained reason, although we were dangerously close to the enemy, we were not called upon to fire until 1515 hrs on the 5th.

We stayed at the Mouen position that night in the midst of what had previously been a strong German entrenched position; lying around the gun position was abandoned and wrecked German equipment – halftracks, wireless trucks, sundry vehicles and kit – interspersed with a few dead bodies. It was a dark and forbidding place and our natural apprehension was increased by the knowledge that the Germans had only pulled back a short distance, and were dangerously close to us. The Troop's nerves were on edge as there did not appear to be any of our own forces nearby to protect us (I discovered later that we were, in fact, temporarily isolated and cut off from any other units). The Troop was alone on the battlefield and out on a limb in a most exposed position. I fully expected an enemy attack at any

65

moment and took what precautions were available to safeguard the Troop.

In this spooky situation, the strain of keeping going over such a prolonged period was taking its effect on me. The stress of combining three of my jobs (BSM, Troop Leader and GPO) was taking its toll to the extent that I was completely exhausted and my legs would not do what my tired brain ordered. Over the past ten days I had had only a few hours sleep. While others could snatch an hour or two here and there, my jobs kept me on the move keeping check on ammunition and rations, bringing the gun records up to date, moving the guns from one position to another, and a multitude of other administrative and gunnery duties, as well as seeing to the welfare of the men.

This night (5/6 July) I was due to be night-duty Relief GPO, but Charles Coad generously offered to stand in for me although he was fast approaching the same state. So while the rest of the Troop peered apprehensively into the dark and damp night, expecting a local attack at any moment, to which we would have had little chance if it came to hand-to-hand fighting (the enemy was as close as a hundred yards away), I simply lay down on the cold wet ground, exactly as I was without any form of cover from the drizzling rain, and passed immediately into unconsciousness. A short while later the agitated Signals Sergeant, Bill Blaber, woke me up and, peering at me with incredulity, spluttered, 'How could you go off to sleep with the bloody Boche only a few yards away?' I said it was very easy. You just lay down and closed your eyes!

Dawn on 6 July was most welcome and our non-firing role continued until eight o'clock in the evening of the 7th, when I was ordered to move the guns further back (with some feelings of relief) and came into action in open country south of the road, north-west of Cheux and west of St Mauvieu (9068), where we immediately resumed firing at fairly long range (relatively speaking, for in this battle anything over 2,000 yards was long range) into Bougy (934608) in the Odon valley in support of the 43rd Wessex Division. We also fired to obliterate an enemy observation post (at 933611) located in open country south-east of Gavrus. That day we watched the RAF bomb Caen, heralding the start of another battle for Caen, code-named Operation Charnwood, in which we only played a fringe role.

Shortly after that evening shoot I received a warning that I was to move the guns to the southern outskirts of Les Saulets (9069) west of Norrey-en-Bessin (wherever we went we seemed to end up at 'Stonk Alley' near

Norrey). The next day, at 0830 hrs, the order came to move to this position at 1250 hrs. As it was believed that the area was mined (by whom, we knew not), we were equipped with mine detectors. 'H' Battery then fired its eight guns again into the Gavrus area (925612). The evening's activities proved to be somewhat intense – as requests for DF and HF tasks came in at 1915 hrs, Don Troop fired a total of 327 rounds (3.65 tons of high explosive).

On 9 July, I was ordered to shift the guns southwards a few yards to our old position at 9068, where the area was fairly well populated by troops from various other units, our task being to support another attack by 43rd Wessex Division on Hill 112 – Operation Jupiter. The barrage began at 0430 hrs on the 10th, and the scale of it, as far as we were concerned, can be judged by the delivery beforehand of 400 rounds per gun, in addition to the sixty or so normally carried on each gun. Shortly after midday, at 1224 hrs, we fired into a concentration of about 100 enemy tanks at Esquay (950610) south-west of Hill 112. On the 11th, I recorded that all my guns had fired over 100 rpg that day, but still the enemy was observed forming up at Maltot (9862) for a further attack. On this position I was relieved of my acting roles, as a new officer, Second Lieutenant Coughborough, joined us. We stayed in this uncomfortable position a few days until 15 July.

At 1100 hrs on Monday, 15 July, the Battery was at long last pulled out of the line for rest and maintenance. We were directed to a position north-west of Brettville l'Orgueilleuse, close to Ste-Croix-Grand-Tonne, north of the Caen–Bayeux road (N13) to await Operation Goodwood. 13th RHA as a whole had moved eight times or more in fourteen days to get closer to its targets (Don Troop moves were more numerous), and, apart from one day, had been continuously in action every day and night.

# Chapter 10

# Operation Goodwood

—⁓—

Operation Goodwood has passed into history as being the last and greatest tank battle fought by the British Army, and is used, I believe, as a text in modern military studies. To put it into perspective, the outcome of that battle was that the 11th Armoured Division, of which we were a part, lost 400 tanks destroyed or incapacitated in three days of fighting, many of the casualties occurring in the first two days.

At troop level, I had little idea of what was afoot, or what our role might be. I always felt that this lack of downward communication was not beneficial – after all, we were the chaps who had to do what the planners had in mind. I was not alone in thinking that the least they could have done was to give us some idea of likely events as they directly affected us, within the limits of security, of course. So it was with Goodwood as it was with Epsom. The more I read about this epic battle, the more I learn that most troops at the sharp end had little idea of the 'big picture'. It was simply a case of 'Prepare to Move', Take Post' and 'Fire', with all that entails.

The most that I could glean was that we were to take part in a tank operation led by 29th Armoured Brigade of 11th Armoured Division, but its place in the wider order of things was not known to me – even the officers, when pressed, knew little more. The first inkling of Goodwood came on 15 July when we had a little respite after the rather messy interlude following on from Epsom, and were merely told that 11th Armoured was to prepare itself for another battle. Confirmation came the next day when we were finally withdrawn from the Caen battles. I was given a pitifully short time in which to refuel and rearm the Troop, and with little time for rest as we were to make a night march that very night, 16/17 July.

VIII Corps, at this time, comprised 11th Armoured, 7th Armoured and the Guards Armoured Divisions, with 159 Infantry Brigade being hived off, tasked to mop up the enemy on the western flank. This left the Division with only 29th Armoured Brigade, and pitifully few infantrymen, to lead the Corps attack. Major General 'Pip' Roberts, commanding 11th Armoured, did not agree with this plan, objecting to the loss of 159 Infantry Brigade from the armoured attack, but the Corps Commander said, 'Take it, Pip, or I'll get someone else to lead.' General Roberts had no intention of not leading the attack, but subsequent events appeared to confirm his original misgivings. The Corps as a whole had about 600 tanks, and the 11th Armoured, as chosen leaders in the battle, would enter the fray with the 3rd Royal Tank Regiment (3 RTR) in the lead, supported by 'H' Battery, of which my 'Don' Troop was a part. In front of us the enemy comprised, among others, parts of the 1st SS (Leibstandarte) (Adolf Hitler) Panzer Division.

General Montgomery's strategic objective was to draw major German armoured formations on to the British front and to hold them in the Caen sector while the American Operation Cobra, in which we later took part (Operation Bluecoat), would achieve a breakthrough in the west. Montgomery's order to General Dempsey commanding Second Army was: 'Second Army will retain the ability to operate with a strong armoured force east of the River Orne in the general area between Caen and Falaise. VIII Corps will attack southwards and establish an armoured division in Bretteville-sur-Laize, Vimont, Falaise.' The Goodwood plan was primarily a tank battle, although supporting arms were to play their part. In essence, however, everything depended on the efforts of the three armoured divisions. The area over which this tank battle would take place was thought by the planners to be 'good tank country', but in fact it turned out to be mostly the opposite. The approaches were awkward and constricted and, as we will see, the area was strewn with mines and the way through was hazardous. The aerial bombardment, which preceded the attack, caused hundreds of deep craters, which hindered both the tanks and our guns.

The Goodwood plan entailed the three armoured divisions repositioning themselves north of Caen, crossing the Caen Canal and the River Orne, turning right, and then squeezing through unmarked minefields. It was not the simplest of operations. The Lines of Communication of both the British and American armies led from north (the beaches) to south, but the armour of Goodwood, comprising 900 tanks and 30,000 men, had to move west to east across those lines. It was not easy.

To join in this affray, we were not pulled out of the line until Sunday,

16 July, rendezvousing at Villons-les-Buissons (905740) north of Caen, leaving us little time to refuel and rearm, for that night we were to began one of two dreadful night marches. It was a brief summer's night of light rain and the movement of tanks filled the damp night air with fumes and dust that turned the ground into a greasy mess over which it was difficult to drive. The countryside was shredded with the tide of war, with rubble from the devastated Caen area littering the tortuous roads along which we travelled.

Don Troop moved nose to tail, led by Charles Coad (an excellent nineteen-year-old officer who I liked and respected, and he trusted me – a good combination); he in turn followed the tank in front of him, identified only by a single dim red rear light. I was travelling immediately behind him as Acting Troop Leader; my job was to see that our four guns were keeping up and travelling nose to tail. When the armoured column moved slowly or stopped, as it mostly did, I frequently had to leap out of my Bren carrier and run back to the rear of the Troop to make sure that all was well on the guns. It was a dangerous game to play as the road was thick with men and vehicles. I then had to catch up and jump back in again. Map reading was out of the question because the previously settled features of topography had been rearranged or removed by the tide of battle. One simply followed as closely as one could the single dim rear light of the vehicle in front and hope for the best.

Charles Coad and I were very worried about the men in the Troop. We had come straight out of a three-week battle action to undertake this night march, with no time for rest for the gunners, and it was particularly hard on the drivers – the tanks in front of us, on the other hand, had had the advantage of a few days out of the line (11th Armoured, less ourselves, had spent a few quiet days back in Cully). I wondered if someone higher up knew of this. All our men were dog-tired, and some of the gunners and sergeants had to relieve exhausted drivers. This posed serious questions, because undertaking a difficult night march of this nature, over ground where normal conditions had been destroyed, required all the proven skills of the permanent and specially trained drivers. The road, if one could call it that, was ravaged by craters and abandoned enemy tanks, lorries and guns, and the light rain falling converted the dust into mud.

These conditions required men in each of the Sextons to take turns in driving, with one man acting as a lookout, endeavouring to cajole the relief driver into keeping up with the vehicle in front. The rest of the crew succumbed to sleep on the steel floor plates. But even in these unreal conditions we managed the move without any serious incident, arriving at the holding area south-west of Escoville at 0630 hrs on the 17th at a place south-west of Bieville (943745), just west of the River Orne. The area was where the 6th Airborne Division had landed from their gliders on D-Day and these lay wrecked all around us. It was an awesome sight to see what appeared to be hundreds of tanks lined up ready for the charge. It was not until 1500 hrs in the afternoon of the 17th that the officers learned the details of Operation Goodwood, but by the time this intelligence percolated down to me it was sketchy indeed. All I knew was that 3rd Royal Tanks would front the attack in a south-easterly push, with 'A' Squadron in the van, and my Troop following closely behind.

There was to be yet another night march that evening, but before attempting to get some rest we had to refuel, rearm, have a hot meal, and carry out some much-needed gun and vehicle maintenance, which I had to organize and oversee. That evening, therefore, we prepared to make the second night march in a slightly better order than the first, although this time we were treated to some sporadic German shelling from the Colombelles area that caused me to think that we had been discovered (as we had been). This second night move took us southwards to the east of Caen, Charles Coad leading, arriving at the assembly area in the Orne bridgehead at Beuville (0574) arriving at 0100hrs on Tuesday the 18th.

The scene around us was difficult to forget. The whole of 29th Armoured Brigade was drawn up in full battle array – a veritable sea of tanks, half-tracks, carriers, guns, etc. In a surreal way it was a wonderful sight to see so much force gathered in so small a place. It had been a misty night and as dawn broke at 0545 hrs, and the mist began to clear, in came 1,056 heavy Lancaster and Halifax bombers, flying relatively low and moving ponderously in waves above us. They bombed for forty-five minutes and were followed by 1,021 American bombers, together providing two and a half hours of intense destruction. We watched this fiendish operation with awe. With over 7,000 tons of high explosive raining down on the German positions, the air was filled with brown dust, smoke and debris. The earth shook and combined with the noise, the scene was indescribable. The Germans were terrified and I could not imagine anyone surviving under it. When later we cautiously passed through the bombed area, there was nothing but a scene of devastation. We even saw a German 52-ton Tiger tank turned upside down by the force of the bomb blasts. The main recipients of this aerial attack were the 16th Luftwaffe Division and the 21st SS Panzer Division.

In front was about 5 miles of utter devastation, the vast open field resembling a moonscape because of the numerous interlocking bomb craters. In dry, bright weather we slowly moved off towards the Start Line south-west of Escoville (115705), following immediately behind 3 RTR (thirty-eight tanks) and alongside a platoon of the 8th Rifle Brigade in their Bren carriers, carefully making our way through the minefields, pausing at about 0700 hrs. 'H' hour for our massive tank attack to begin was 0745hrs when an intensive artillery barrage would continue on from the bombing – 700 guns sited somewhere behind us opened up with a tremendous roar over a short front of 2,000 yards, advancing by lifts each of 150 yards.

We moved off on time (0745 hrs) in box formation and reached an open area of pasture clouded in smoke and dust east of Cuverville (115705), from which area came a serious amount of enemy anti-tank fire from guns hidden in the hedgerows, but 3 RTR cleared it with their machine guns. Both Cuverville and Demouville were heavily fortified German defences, and although they suffered grievously from the bombing, there were still sufficient of the enemy left to cause us to be apprehensive as we trundled past them on the east side. When our advance took us beyond the minefield we had to close up tightly, operating on a small front of about 1,000 yards. Then, after leaving the minefields behind us, 3 RTR saw 5 miles of open country in front of them, but the frontage of attack closed down to 700 yards, narrowing down so that the tanks were moving in single file.

By this time our tiredness was replaced with a surge of adrenaline as the panorama of battle enveloped us. The sun was coming up, the day was warm, and the corn and wheat fields were 3 to 10 feet high (proving good cover for enemy snipers left behind). This rustic scene imbued us with a feeling of excitement, though shortly it was to be rudely shattered. For the moment our gun support was not required, and apart from instinctively ducking as something nasty exploded fairly close, we drove slowly and carefully about 2 to 3 miles an hour towards the embanked Caen-Troarn railway line that lay directly across our path, but still keeping close to the creeping artillery barrage. We arrived at this position at 0805 hrs. At 0850 the artillery barrage from across the Orne River lifted to the south-west (our Centre Line), but the leading tanks, with us close behind, could not keep pace with the forward sweep of the barrage due to shelling from the 503rd Heavy Panzer Battalion.

By this time we were east and south of the fortified village of

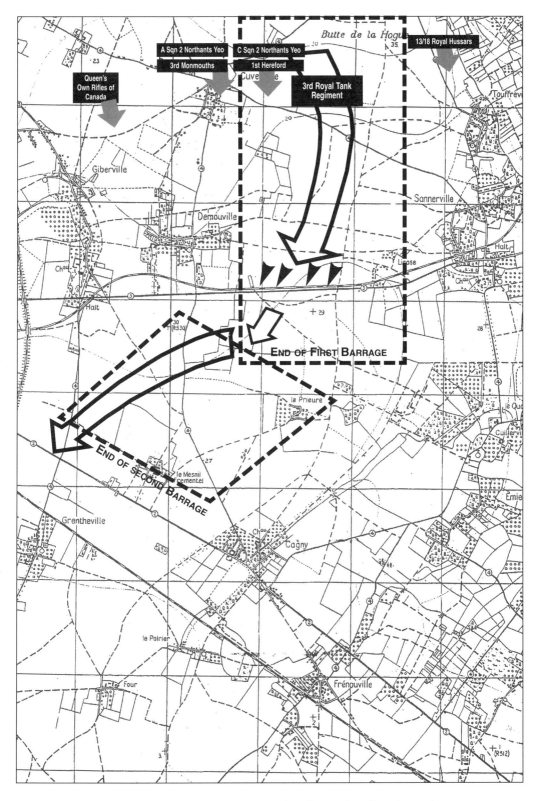

The advance of 3RTR (supported by 'Don' Troop) in Operation Goodwood. *(Courtesy of Ian Daglish))*

Demouville. At about 0900hrs the barrage ended as the guns behind us ran out of range. At 1000hrs we came into our first action of this great battle south of Demouville and west of Emieville (0965), north of the Caen-Troan railway line, where we were harassed by enemy fire, but with only one casualty (Gunner Barnes). We took seventy prisoners who did not look very pleased about it, then after two quick shoots moved on towards the embanked railway.

The railway embankment was a steep six-foot obstacle, rising sharply from the ground, along the top of which ran two sets of rail tracks. At the point where we were expected to cross over, the lines ran straight mainly on an east-west axis. It was a formidable obstacle and was something outside our experience. The point that struck me was that although we were in possession, as it were, of the length immediately facing us, both ends to the right and left were still enemy-occupied territory, albeit some distance away. We had visions, therefore, of German tanks or anti-tank guns stationed at each end picking us off one by one as we clambered over the embankment. To the east were positioned twenty-two Panzer Mk IVs south of Sannerville, with to the west a company of self-propelled guns, and we were nicely placed in between them, but we managed to get over to the other side without too much trouble. 3 RTR solved some of the problems of the embankment facing them by employing an Armoured Vehicle Royal Engineers (AVRE) to fire one of its 290mm petard mortars, comprising 40 lb of high explosive, nicknamed 'Flying Dustbins', to blow gaps in the embankment. Unfortunately, this useful facility was denied us as we were a little off centre in relation to the route of the tanks.

When it was our turn to get over the embankment, the order to proceed was made more in hope than in expectation, and each Sexton had to wait on the other side until all guns were across. First one Sexton revved up its engine to maximum revolutions, then another, thus adding to the screaming noise emanating from the shells of the barrage whistling overhead and crashing down not all that far in front of us. I was apprehensive, because I knew that unless the guns took the crossing of the embankment straight ahead, there was the possibility that they would roll over sideways and finish upside down. Fortunately, the drivers were sufficiently skilled and the four guns mounted the embankment safely – only to face the problem caused by the steel tracks of the Sextons skidding on the steel railway lines, making the descent on the opposite side a hazardous event indeed.

I watched these manoeuvres with some trepidation and was relieved when my four guns managed to get across safely and without too much harm, but there was still the Troop's Command Post vehicle, an American White half-track, together with my Bren carrier, yet to perform the same feat, and I had strong doubts as to their ability to do so as their engines were not so powerful as the Sextons. As it happened, the half-track had rubber tracks, and so did very well, but I was still on one side of the embankment with the Troop on the other. If I couldn't get across, the Troop would have to move off without us – being alone on a raging battlefield was not an inviting prospect. That particular scenario was yet to come!

My driver, 'Smudger' Smith, had not been idle, and had been working things out in his own mind. He had the idea that we should not start from a stationary position at the foot of the bank like the others, but drive at the embankment from a position 20 to 30 yards away. It would be bumpy, but he thought the momentum would allow the engine to do the rest (the Ford engine of the Bren carrier, of 85 bhp and a maximum of 3,000 rpm, was not so powerful as those of the Sextons), especially if he took the same routes of the tanks and the Sextons, because they had chewed up the ground, thus making the surface non-adhesive. I agreed with Driver Smith, of course – one does not argue with a skilled driver who has drawn his own conclusions. We settled in the carrier in a manner that would hopefully allow us to retain our presence there and not be thrown out, and off we went.

Smith drove the short distance to the bank at half speed in first gear and when he reached the steep foot of the bank he accelerated to maximum revs. I was thrown back onto the bulkhead and only escaped being deposited on the inside rear of the carrier by holding on grimly to the Browning machine gun mounted in front of me. All I could see was the sky. Then we crashed down heavily onto the railway tracks and began to skid sideways before sliding down the other side with the brakes full on. Smith[1] got a congratulatory cheer from his fellow drivers, while I rubbed a bruised back. Fortunately, I didn't realize then what part that self-same embankment would play in the nightmare yet to come.

Stretched out in front was a more or less flat open cornfield, quite extensive in area, and to our immediate front 3 RTR were already engaging

---

1 Gunner Smith drove my Bren carrier many miles through many adventures, but months later, in Holland, he had the misfortune to drive over a mine and was killed instantly.

targets, at the same time taking incoming enemy fire. The Germans had dug in their enormous Tiger Mk VI tanks and self-propelled guns on the Borguebus Ridge, and were taking dreadful toll of 3 RTR's tanks. They were being destroyed or immobilized one by one; as each one became disabled, it issued volumes of black smoke before exploding into flames. Not for nothing were Shermans called 'Tommy Cookers' by the Germans ('Ronsons' by us). It was heart breaking to see some surviving tank crews, blackened, horribly burnt, clothes smouldering, staggering back to find some sort of shelter. This slaughter came from the 1st SS Panzer Division which had at its disposal, as I later learnt, forty-six Tiger Mk VI and Panther Mk V tanks, together with twenty self-propelled guns, supported by the 272nd Infantry Division.

It was about this time that I witnessed a heroic act in the rescue of a wounded comrade. Sergeant Dunbar was the Signals Sergeant of 'I' Battery and I saw him over to my right walking upright, apparently unconcerned, through waist-high corn, under shell and machine-gun fire, to rescue someone who had been wounded. He was awarded the Military Medal. He was an extraordinary man who had been the Chief of Staff to the Government Forces in the Spanish Civil War and was described by Aneurin Bevan in the House of Commons as 'the man who flung 150,000 men across Elbro'. He was offered, and refused, an immediate commission. After the war he was found drowned in the sea off Milford-on-Sea in Hampshire.

I was now in the thick of the battle, being harassed by direct and indirect shell and mortar fire falling all around us. Still on the move, we edged forward yard by yard until we came into our first action about 300 yards south of the railway embankment (0965), and began firing in accordance with orders coming from up front. The guns were firing as quickly as they could be loaded and the German shelled us in return. Our shooting was so quick and intense, with the gunners working flat out, that the action kept my mind off the effects of enemy shelling, although the shelling and mortaring was too close for comfort. The immediate battlefield was by now almost obliterated by smoke and dust billowing about, punctuated by the angry red flames of burning tanks, exploding shells and anything else that could burn going off around us. There were many dead and wounded Germans mixed up with our own casualties, and the cries of the wounded were pitiful to hear. Even so, some surviving Germans lying in the waist-high corn were brave enough to continue sniping all and sundry, and bullets whizzed around like angry bees. We were lucky not to have any casualties at that time.

On one occasion during this maelstrom of continuous fire emanating from both sides, I was able to deduce that, whoever of the enemy might have us in direct sight, might be holed up in a cottage some 400 yards to our left front. I got permission from Charles Coad (the GPO) to disengage No. 4 gun of 'H' subsection from collective Troop firing, and directed Sgt Barratt to fire over open sights at the building in question. So fierce and dangerous was the action all around us that his gunlayer appeared to be in a state of hysterical excitement, and at 400 yards he missed hitting a sizeable building. Normally, he could hit a tank at 1,500 yards without giving it another thought. His next round, however, did the trick but his reputation as an ace gunlayer was dented somewhat in subsequent banter.

I had been kept busy all this time running from gun to gun and to the Troop Command Post checking and rearranging ammunition stocks (some guns fired more shells than their neighbours), noting that ammunition supply trucks might be held up, unable to negotiate the first railway embankment. At the same time I tried to comply with many and fierce requests from the harassed gun sergeants who seemed to think I had nothing better to do than to stroll around the gun position. More often than not, guns had to be relaid (they only had 4 degrees of traverse each way), because the continual twisting and turning on their tracks to conform to the diverse directions of fire, distorted the parallelism of the Troop as a whole. This state was usually discovered by my frequent compass checks taken from behind the guns.

This momentous morning wore on and at 1000 hrs I assisted in moving position near to Grentheville (0864). To do so we had to cross the second lateral railway line in front of us, but this time 3 RTR had discovered a tunnel of sorts underneath the railway lines, thereafter known by all as 'The Drain', and we were able to pass through without incident. We appeared to be moving on the left flank of 3 RTR, for they were moving along the west side of the railway line west of Soliers, probing in the direction of Bras, whilst we were positioned midway northwards of Grentheville and Le Poirer, so we were firing on about 200 degrees south-west. The resisting Germans were intent on not giving way and the fighting became more intense, with the tanks making little or no progress.

The battlefield by now began to resemble scenes from the First World War, with flames from burning tanks, billowing plumes of smoke and debris, and metal splinters flying in every direction; badly wounded tankers were lying amidst the corn or struggling to find shelter. Our gunners slaved away stripped to the waist, smoke-blackened and dishevelled. The earth shook and the noise was stupefying, making the passage of orders from the Command Post to the guns a matter of great difficulty, and often I had to act as a runner to convey the requisite fire orders. This was not, however, the end of things.

We were being shelled by fire directed from an enemy observation post some 300 yards away in another railway embankment that ran north to south from Caen to Borguebus and beyond. We shelled it over open sights, destroyed it and captured the German observation officer. We also took seventy prisoners from a shattered infantry regiment. We were not immune from retaliation, however, and almost immediately Sergeant Davies of 'E' subsection was hit in the neck and shoulder, and Second Lieutenant Coughbrough, our Troop Leader, was wounded.

The Battery FOOs up with the leading tanks were having a hectic time, which meant that our responses at the guns were equally frenetic. There were many quick shoots, mostly on prearranged concentrations (twenty-four guns firing in unison), and on occasions we had to fire smoke shells to get 3 RTR out of trouble. A German counter-attack was mounted against us, on which we brought down several 'stonks' forcing them to pull back. A *Nebelwerfer* battery was silenced.

In these frantic actions, in addition to the wounds of Davies and Coughbrough incurred at the gun position, Captain Vivian's tank (C , Troop) up front was hit and he died of wounds within minutes. Gunner E.T. Jones was also killed in action, and Gunners Gillham and Snowden were wounded, as was Captain Bicket.

When Sergeant Davies was wounded, it began a day of strange occurrences. Davies was in dire trouble. A sniper's bullet, or it may have been a shell fragment, had entered the lower part of his neck and lodged in his shoulder, causing him agonizing pain. A phial of morphine was pumped into him but its effects were only partial. It was clear that he had to be taken quickly to the Regimental Aid Post (RAP), wherever that might be. And that was my job.

It so happened that when we had been at Kilham in East Yorkshire a couple of months earlier, realizing that my Bren carrier was to accommodate the Troop's only stretcher, I conceived the idea of having brackets welded onto the front and rear bulkheads in the form of inverted stirrups to accommodate the stretcher handles when the stretcher was opened up. That idea was now to bear fruit. It took six of us to get Davies out of the Sexton and onto the stretcher along and above the engine of the carrier. It fell to me to evacuate him by taking him to the first medical facility (the RAP) from whence he would go to a Casualty Clearing Station and then to a hospital. The immediate problem was that no one, least of all myself, had the slightest idea where the RAP was.

The RAP was wherever the Regiment's Medical Officer (RMO) decided to park his four-wheeled truck, and it took no great intelligence to work out that such a vehicle could not surmount the railway embankment that had given us all so much trouble. My first task therefore was to go back over that obstacle and hunt around on the other side for the RAP. I set off most carefully. Driver Smith manoeuvred the carrier slowly, twisting and turning to avoid as much as possible bomb and shell craters, dead bodies, burning tanks and exploding shells, with the carrier lurching alarmingly this way and that. The other occupant of the carrier was Lance Bombardier Muscoe, the Troop's indefatigable vehicle fitter, who habitually rode with me. His immediate concern was to see that Davies did not slide off the stretcher during these wild manoeuvres.

The journey back to the embankment was awful. The cornfield was still under shell and mortar fire, and snipers' bullets whistled around. Davies was coming out of his sedation, his groans from the pain became more vocal and we felt bad about it because of the slow progress we had to make. We were now somewhere midway between the guns and the railway embankment, when Driver Smith pulled up. He'd spotted something and, drawing my attention to it, I could see a wounded man lying across our path. I cautiously dismounted, went over to investigate and found it to be Gunner E.T. Jones. He was largely unconscious with what appeared to be a nasty throat wound. This was confusing. What was he doing there all alone? Had he been abandoned? What sort of duty had he been performing alone on a seething battlefield out of contact with his unit? I felt sure that no one in my Battery would have abandoned a wounded colleague, but there seemed to be no answer to our questions. He was not even wearing the emergency dressing that we all carried. That mystery was never solved. I used the dressings taken from Smith, Muscoe and myself, and did what we could to keep the wound covered.

The next problem was what to do with Jones? We realized that there was no room in the carrier for him. The stretcher took up all the space on the near side of the engine and Muscoe had to stand up on the other side just to keep Davies on the stretcher. I whispered in Jones's ear that I would come back for him as soon as I had delivered Davies to the RAP, but I think he was too close to death to understand. We covered him with a blanket before Muscoe took an iron stake from his kit, drove it into the ground by the side of the wounded man and put Jones's hat on it in the hope that no one would run over him. We then set off for the embankment.

Our approach to the railway embankment was a hazardous affair. We steered between burning tanks, the black smoke billowing from them choking in our throats. We tried to keep clear of these tanks as best we could, as some of them tended to disintegrate unpredictably as their ammunition exploded. We eventually reached the foot of the dreaded embankment, but how were we to get over to the other side? It will be recalled that on the previous occasion Smith had charged the bank to gain momentum for the ascent, but there was no possibility of doing that now with Davies lying prone on the stretcher in great pain. There was no alternative but to start from scratch, as it were, and hope for the best. Smith selected first gear and pressed hard on the accelerator. The engine screamed as he released the brake and the front of the carrier rose pointing to the sky.

The carrier was now at an acute angle and Muscoe had somehow to support Davies on the stretcher by dragging on the wounded man's battledress blouse, whilst I gripped Davies' feet. The carrier did its best, moving up and forward, slipping sideways, then taking a grip on the banked earth, until we reached the top. Sweat poured from Smith's face, but there was worse to follow. For a moment, the carrier stood poised at an angle pointing skywards, then it crashed down horizontally on to the railway tracks. Poor old Davies! His head was to the rear of the carrier, so that when we climbed the bank his body up-ended, head down, causing more blood to spurt from his wound. We crashed down on to the railway lines, but the jolting was too much for him and he fainted from the pain. It seemed to be easier going down the other side as Muscoe and I had got the hang of holding Davies down, keeping him more or less stable.

Then we had the day's first piece of luck, for without knowing it we had crossed the embankment at precisely the point where the Doctor had positioned the RAP. It was a horrifying scene. His truck was at the foot of the embankment, shielded from the battle raging on the other side, but on the ground around him was a sea of wounded and dead men. I had to wait a while as the MO moved from man to man pumping morphine into them, whilst his orderly (whose unfortunate name was Lance Bombardier Dedman) put tabs on the dead and wounded, and applied rudimentary bandages where possible. Neither was the RAP exclusively for Allied forces. There seemed to be as many Germans lying there as there were British, either dead or just alive. Then it was our turn and, after giving the Doctor a brief explanation of Davies' condition, the MO stuck in his needle of morphine, and said there was nothing more that he or I could do. It took some months for Sergeant Davies to recover in England, although I believe he lost an arm.

I had to wait a few minutes while Smith refuelled from a 4-gallon can of petrol, so I looked around; two matters caught my attention. One concerned a wounded German. He was just a boy, probably no more than fifteen or sixteen, and his left leg was shattered. He lay there, silent and uncomplaining. His pitiful eyes followed me around. He wanted to say something, but couldn't. I stood by him until I could bear it no longer and turned away. The same thought went through my mind each time I had contact with a dead or wounded man, friend or foe. Someone back home – mother, father, brothers, sisters, wives and children – might happily be engaged in ordinary daily pursuits, not knowing that at that precise moment their loved one lay alone on the battlefield, dead or badly wounded.

I tried to put these sad thoughts out of my mind, although it didn't quieten the fear that one day or even one hour soon I might be in the same unfortunate position. I therefore directed my attention to the matter of what to do next. Alongside the RAP a convoy of wheeled armoured lorries of the Royal Army Service Corps was drawn up, stuck there until someone could find a way of getting them over the embankment. It occurred to me that with a bit of luck they might conceivably be carrying 25-pdr ammunition and that I might be able to relieve them of some of it. I hadn't taken into account, though, the difficulty this would entail.

I approached one of the drivers and put my request to him. Certainly, he was carrying 25-pdr shells, but he refused to part with any because he had to deliver them to a particular regiment, and I wasn't from that regiment. It didn't take me long to find a way around that difficulty. I simply asked another driver what regiment he was heading for – it wasn't mine, but I said it was, and I was able to load the carrier with eight boxes of 25-pdr shells, four to a box, each box weighing about a hundredweight.

My crazy idea was to take this ammunition back to where we had left Jones, unload, take Jones to the RAP, come back, reload, and then rejoin the Troop. But I know that the best laid plans of mice and men 'oft gang aglae', as the Hibernian saying goes.

Meanwhile, Driver Smith had located an easier part of the embankment to cross over, but we did so with some difficulty due to the added weight of the ammunition in the carrier. The journey back was not any easier. The shelling by the Germans seemed to be more intense and we thought we had inadvertently run into some sort of direct enemy intent. They were clearly firing on this part of the cornfield, probably to prevent reserves being brought forward, as we entered the thick of it. Luck was with us, however, and we reached Jones's position marked by the helmet and stake, but there was no Jones! Neither was there anyone else. The mystery deepened. Why was he there in the first place and why was he not there now? Had he crawled somewhere else? No, he was too badly hurt for that. I looked around, and apart from the dead and the dying, there was no living soul in sight. I never found any explanation for this small but tragic event.

I set off to return to the Troop on the other side of the second railway line where we had left them. The three of us were by now very tired, hungry and thirsty, and somewhat bedraggled. Our return would bring some relief. Driver Smith carefully picked his way through the ravaged cornfield and approached 'The Drain' leading to the Troop position, but as we reached there and passed into the open cornfield that we had left earlier that day, not a gun was in sight. The Troop had gone and there was no forwarding address! All that remained of its presence was the debris from each gun – discarded brass shell cases, coloured bags of cordite and empty boxes.

The situation was surreal. Gunner Jones had mysteriously disappeared and Don Troop appeared to have done the same. Could there be some malevolent spirit dogging our footsteps? In my fevered imagination, I even had the fleeting thought that we might actually be dead and were now confined to some sort of purgatory. The cacophonic and erupting environment was certainly amenable to these tortured musings.

I looked around for someone we might turn to for assistance, but apart from the enemy's attempts to rearrange the surface of the earth, the battlefield seemed to be devoid of any signs of intelligent life. There was plenty of other activity, however, for smouldering tanks and other forms of damaged hardware littered the field. Had the Troop moved forward, sideways or even backwards? we pondered. There were no means of telling and not for the first time we were alone in the most unpleasant of circumstances.

Something had to be done; we couldn't just stay there hoping for the best. I decided against going forward as that was where a tank battle was taking place, with tanks fighting tanks. From what I could see and hear, it would be madness to enter into that maelstrom on the off chance of finding four guns, although my instinct told me that if they were anywhere, that is where they would be. What made the making of decisions worse was that we had no wireless set on board. It had been removed in the early part of the morning for some reason and in the urgency of evacuating Davies the set had not been replaced. The only alternative action left to me was to reconnoitre the area in the wild hope of making contact with the Troop.

I decided to go north-east, back in the direction of the dreaded first railway line. My starting-off point was the Troop's original position that was immediately south of Grentheville (0864), just south of the second railway line. I was unaware at the time that strong German defences were established in Cagny (1064) and le Prieure (1063), with which we were soon to come in contact. We moved around slowly, scanning the battlefield and listening for the unmistakeable crack of 25-pdrs firing.

I edged towards Le Mesnil Frementel, which had been heavily knocked about but was still in enemy hands, when I came across a small agricultural quarry lined with trees and scrub. There, at last, was some sign of life. A very young British Second Lieutenant, who looked to be no more than fourteen, flagged me down. He was distressed and incoherent, and for a while I couldn't understand what he was saying over the noise around us. Fortunately another man emerged and explained that their scout car was stranded in the quarry, and couldn't get out. Sure enough, there was the vehicle at the bottom of the quarry, and, so far as I could gather, shells landing close to it had either blasted it there, or it had been driven in for shelter and got stuck. It seemed to be unnecessary to enquire further. Lance Bombardier Muscoe, ever resourceful, attached drag ropes, and with a lot of effort on Driver Smith's part we pulled them out. After the vehicle was on level ground, I asked the young officer if, in his travels, he had come across a Troop of self-propelled 25-pdrs. He was plainly shell-shocked and to our astonishment he immediately jumped into the scout car, and without offering a word of thanks, shot off to Heaven knows where.

This entertaining interlude cheered us up a little and we continued on our quest. We had not gone far when help at last seemed on hand. Parked in front of us was a half-track and standing beside it was Captain 'Bunny' Davis, our Regimental Adjutant. He and his crew were alone and as he stood there I felt a surge of relief. He was resolute and calm, festooned with headphones and microphones, holding a map in his hands. Bedraggled and blackened, I went up to him and saluted. I explained what we had been up to and asked if he could tell me the whereabouts of Don Troop? I thought that if he didn't know, no one would. He said he was not sure, peering at his map, but he gave me a map reference (105645) of where he thought they might be. I plotted this on my map, noting that the location was on the western extremity of Cagny (107646). As we moved away much relieved, I could see in front of me the profile of a line of trees about a mile away, beyond which was the village of Cagny. It was not only under attack, with a pall of smoke hovering over it, but it was also busily retaliating.

I had no reason to doubt the Adjutant's guesswork, so I directed Driver Smith to push eastwards through a belt of small trees, to face a large flat expanse of pasture extending up to Cagny less than a mile away. We proceeded cautiously, nevertheless, with the feeling of relief overcoming pangs of hunger and exhaustion. At the same time, I was painfully aware that the scene we were about to enter was by no means peaceful, with shells screaming low over our heads in *both directions.*

What I didn't know was that we were driving right through the middle of a furious tank battle. Behind us were the tanks of the Fife and Forfar Yeomanry, and to our left and right fronts on the edge of Cagny were the dreaded 88mm anti-aircraft guns. Their role was to defend Caen against Allied bombers, but they now found themselves converted into anti-tank guns. It has since passed into legend that the commander of the 88mm guns initially refused the orders of Colonel Hans von Luck, but the Colonel produced a revolver and said, in effect, 'A bullet or a Knight's Cross.'[2] The orders were accepted and von Luck's own heavy Tiger tanks, together with Major Becker's *Sturmgeshutz* heavy guns, further augmented this hostile defensive screen – and we were heading directly into the muzzles of those guns only 500 or 600 yards away!

Then it seemed that Divine Providence intervened on our behalf, for there seemed to be no other explanation. The distance between the enemy

---

2 For a fuller account of this episode see Dunphie, Christopher, *Operation Goodwood*, Pen & Sword Books, 2004, pp. 78-9.

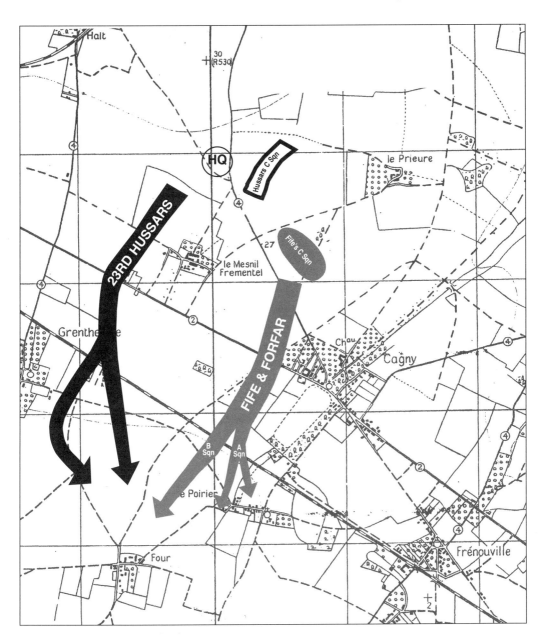

Cagny, showing the ground over which the author ventured
in his Bren gun carrier. (*Courtesy of Ian Daglish*)

guns and us was slowly shortening and it would only be a matter of a few minutes before we were on top of them. I could now clearly see the muzzle flashes of the four 88s and the Sturmgesshutz self-propelled heavy guns. I was taking us to almost certain oblivion. That is where Providence took a hand. The Ford engine of the Bren carrier suddenly stalled and brought the carrier to a shuddering halt. What could otherwise have been an irritation was a godsend, momentarily saving us from instant destruction.

The cylinder block of the tortured engine had been put under extreme pressure throughout this fraught day and was glowing red hot. There was nothing that even Muscoe, the Troop's vehicle mechanic, could do about it. So there we were, stationary on a battlefield, with enemy 88mm guns pointing more or less directly at us from a few hundred yards away, and our own tanks and artillery a similar distance behind us, in turn, firing at them. It was this providential halt that saved our lives. The Germans, for reasons unknown to us, left us alone, although that was not the impression we gained at the time. They might even have thought that we had been hit. High-explosive and armour-piercing shells came over and around us from both sides in a screaming and screeching cacophony of noise, deafening us and covering us in dust and debris. All we could do was to sit there and await death.

It was the Germans who eventually won this particular tank battle, for almost all the tanks of the Fife and Forfar Yeomanry behind us were either destroyed or disabled by the formidable 88s. The 23rd Hussars, who were in the vicinity, joined in the affray, but they too suffered grievously in much the same way.

There was death and destruction wherever one looked on this battlefield and I was painfully aware that we were sitting on a time bomb, as the carrier was loaded with the high-explosive 25-pdr shells I had picked up at the RAP. A hit on the carrier of any sort would have blown us all to smithereens. Driver Smith, crouching down behind his steering wheel, was heard to mutter glumly, 'Well, if they hit us, we shan't know much about it.' I wasn't comforted by his prognosis.

During this surreal scenario, Lance Bombardier Muscoe, sitting behind me on boxes filled with high explosive, occupied himself with matters mechanical, making desperate efforts to restart the engine, but he could do nothing until it cooled. The heat not only made it impossible to touch it, but it also evaporated the petrol. Eventually, and it must have been half an hour or so, his efforts prevailed, as he somehow got the engine to splutter spasmodically. Driver Smith immediately engaged reverse gear, and at a speed of about 2 miles per hour, backed to what had been our front line. The engine coughed and stopped then restarted itself, and we limped back towards the hedgerow trees that had supposedly shielded the Fife and ForFars. We were helped by the dense clouds of billowing black smoke coming from burning tanks. Smith backed the carrier into a thin line of trees, where we were able to turn around and proceed cautiously in forward gear.

By now, this eventful day was drawing to a close, and we still hadn't located the Troop, or, indeed, any friendly units (only dead ones). Then, because I could think of nothing else, I decided to return to the original vacated gun position where we had last seen them, in the hope that they might possibly have sent someone out to find us. We passed under 'The Drain' of the second railway line, noting that the intensity of battle we had previously witnessed had waned somewhat, and that the dense smoke cover had now broken up into fragmented drifting black clouds. Then, to my astonishment and unbelievable relief, there, in front of our very eyes, as the smoke cleared, was the missing Troop! They had moved only a few hundred yards from the position we had left, to occupy a more forward position midway between Four and Soliers, but we had failed to see them the first time because of the poor visibility and the battle prevailing there.

It was now late afternoon and we had been away for several hours, during which time the Troop had been continuously in action. My small contribution of eight boxes of 25-pdr shells – a meagre thirty-two rounds transported in somewhat unusual conditions – was most welcome. Eight shells each is not much, but if you are short of ammunition, it is a lot. By 1800 hrs, our firing slackened as the remnants of 3 RTR, whom we were supporting, ran out of ammunition and so remained idle for a while.

The explanations for our absence from the gun position were accepted and the Command Post Officer deduced that, in our wanderings, we had never been more than half a mile away from the Troop. But half a mile in the midst of tank battles can be quite a distance. Some of the men, however, uncharitably, but not unkindly, suggested that we had 'buggered off'. I learned that during the time we were away, the Germans had attacked 29th Armoured Brigade at 1300, 1445, 1545 and 1615 hrs, keeping 'Don' Troop fully engaged. At 2020 hrs the village of Soliers was infiltrated by German armour and all British guns in range put up a huge artillery barrage, but in vain as six Tiger Mk VI tanks and five Panther Mk

V tanks came out of the village of Bras and attacked 3 RTR, for whom we had to give our total attention and support, at the same time taking our share of the enemy's fire. It was not until 2300 hrs on the first day of Goodwood (the 18th) that the battle died down. By this time 11th Armoured Division had lost 126 tanks destroyed or disabled, and 521 men. The remaining tanks withdrew for the night and laagered by the railway line 1,200 yards south-west of Grentheville.

The night of 18/19 July brought little respite. Although the tanks remaining operational from the day's disasters were temporarily withdrawn, we had to remain in action to maintain supporting fire to beat off counter-attacks and break up enemy formations.

The next day the fragmented configuration of the battlefield caused the Troop to move, this time to Cheux, to a position that was more or less the same as the one we occupied during Operation Epsom. We initially supported 29th Armoured Brigade, especially 3 RTR who were attacking Bras (0663), but we were heavily shelled in return. We had to stick it out, however, as the battle was now intense, and we remained in that uncomfortable position until 1600 hrs when 3 RTR again attacked Bras and Hubert Folie, entering Bras at 1710 hrs. To our consternation we found ourselves isolated, being the only gun battery in the area, and we stayed there until 1600 hrs on the 20th when at last we came out of action. By now, we were all dead tired and hungry.

We took shelter for the night in the lee of the second railway embankment, where we could refuel and rearm. Some food was available, and the gunners and drivers tried to get some much-needed rest. Unfortunately the hot weather, which had been heavy and sullen all day, broke into a violent thunderstorm, from which we had little shelter from the pouring rain, which did nothing to relieve the momentous events of the day. Then, just to be perverse, the Luftwaffe came over and bombed the unfortunate Fife and Forfar Yeomanry and Divisional Headquarters nearby, causing more casualties. The 11th Armoured Division was by now battered and mauled, having lost 191 tanks and suffered 731 casualties during the day. The remnants withdrew from the battlefield, but we stayed in action.

The rain continued over into the next day and whilst nominally in action on the north side of the second railway line (Caen–Vimont), it was possible to take stock of our surroundings. Casualties had to be replaced and jobs moved around. For myself, while still retaining the rank of

Warrant Officer, I formally became, in the absence of the wounded Second Lieutenant Coughborough, Acting Troop Leader (TLD) and Relief Gun Position Officer (GPO), with a bit of Forward Observation Officer thrown in. These were the four jobs I had been doing since Epsom. It was also for us the end of Operation Goodwood. Goodwood has gone down in history as the greatest British tank battle, ranking with the famous (or infamous) Kursk tank battle fought on the Russian front. In the early hours of the 23rd, we had orders to move out of the line to Authie, north-west of Caen, and north of the N13 (as it became), so beginning for me another small adventure.

# Chapter 11

# Authie

─⟋⟍─

Sgt Barratt's Sexton ('H' subsection) developed some trouble with its gears and it was felt that not only could it not keep pace with the others, but also, because of the vehicle's malfunction, it would probably be unable to negotiate any barriers, particularly railway embankments. I was therefore detailed to take charge of it and to find my own way to Authie. My Bren carrier was not available to me as it was required to transport the gun and vehicle fitters, who were now required for other duties. I therefore travelled in the damaged Sexton.

It seemed to me that whatever route I chose to take, it would lead me over bomb and shell cratered ground, through minefields, and over trenches previously occupied by the enemy, but there seemed to be no alternative. I also had to find a way that was not obstructed by railway embankments, knowing that the damaged Sexton would be unable to surmount any angled banks. I therefore set out on a compass bearing leading to Giberville (0968), to the south of which appeared to be a crossing of sorts over the Caen-Troarn railway line that was not embanked. Even if the Sexton had been fully roadworthy, I would have been reluctant to attempt a climb over the dreaded railway embankment. Moreover, although I believed that the route I had chosen was now clear of the enemy, I was soon to be disabused of that unfounded belief.

The disabled Sexton made laborious progress over the tortured ground that had been torn to pieces by bomb and shell craters. Neither was the weather particularly kind, being gloomy and overcast. Caen lay to the west of us and although I believed that it was now in our hands, bullets still swished over and around us. German infantry, lying in the cornfields, were busily sniping at anything that moved – and that included us. We had to keep our heads down. I followed a track bounded on the left by a post and wire fence and it was from that direction that some enemy artillery fire came down, adding to our discomfort. The shelling landed uncomfortably close, which I found to be disconcerting because I thought that either the Canadians or 159 Infantry Brigade had cleared the enemy from this area east of Caen. I began anxiously to wonder whether I was right to choose this particular route.

We pressed on, however, trying to avoid minefields by looking out for the remnants of white tape that had once marked a clear passage through. It was an anxious time, because although I thought that the area to the right of us was relatively free of enemy activity, that was more than could be said of the flat expanse of open land to my left, particularly in the Mondeville area (0760), the outlines of which were visible. Nothing is predictable on a battlefield and what seemed to be a perfectly good route on a map proved not to be the case in reality, for I realized we were actually travelling through enemy-held territory. The area around us was under enemy fire, and we were periodically sniped and mortared. The partly disabled Sexton travelled slowly, mostly in first or second gear, and it seemed to be an eternity before I could find some cover.

I eventually managed to find the main road, the D226, at Cuverville, where I turned left and trundled through the north side of Caen to Herouville, almost as far as Abbeye d'Ardennes, then branched off right to Authie, arriving about 1000 hrs. To my surprise and relief we arrived half an hour before my Battery appeared. It had come the long way round north of Caen, having been able to negotiate the obstacles I had avoided. Some chaps in my Troop pulled my leg in humorous truculence, muttering darkly, 'Whose side are you on?' I hadn't realized when starting off that I had travelled through enemy-held territory, but I was deeply relieved to know I'd got away with it.

The village, or suburb, of Authie was a chosen meeting place for the Division, because in a day or so, as we later learned, we were to go off westwards to begin yet another battle, code-named Operation Bluecoat ('Cobra' for the Americans, with whom we were to make the breakthrough to the River Seine). So for us, that was the end of Operation Goodwood. It had failed to achieve its objectives, but it did make a substantial contribution to the current and ensuing events because it tied up German armour on the British front, leaving the Americans with less armoured opposition to face in the oncoming battle over to the west.

The stay at Authie was a blessed relief. The Troop had now been in direct contact with the enemy forces for four weeks with very little let-up, and the change in the gunners was most noticeable. From being innocents abroad in mid June, the men were now battle-hardened soldiers and

St Lô–Bayeaux

certainly looked the part. Ragged, unshaven, unwashed, short of sleep and in need of a decent meal, we were glad to partake of the 'amenities' of Authie. It appeared to be a small village strung out along a staggered crossroads. It was difficult to believe that only a couple of days ago, the German Army had occupied it intensively for four years.

In the short time of British occupation, mobile baths had been rigged up and a cookhouse established. It was now 23 July and the weather was still not good. I organized an orgy of maintenance, sprucing up the guns and vehicles, with the inevitable and constant tasks of refitting, refuelling and stocking up with ammunition. Sundry articles were 'liberated' from goodness knows where (one didn't ask) and added to the sparse facilities on board. Timber and canvas were in great demand to provide shelter for the gunners. On two of the evenings we spent in Authie, an ENSA dance band, including a comedian, entertained us in the village hall (such luxury!), even though the artistes and ourselves were a little disconcerted by various unfriendly bangs and crashes nearby. The Germans certainly had our range. A certain amount of Troop and Battery reorganization also ensued, with the taking in of new officers and men to replace our casualties, and time had to be spent in introducing them to their new duties.

It is worth noting here, en passant, that in the two days of Operation Goodwood, the 11th Armoured Division, along with others in VIII Corps, had occupied 34 square miles of territory for the loss of 500 tanks and 4,000 men.[1] Fortunately, many of the tank crews survived, but a lot of the tanks did not and had to be replaced, coming from seemingly inexhaustible American stocks. It is sad statistics of this nature that put the battles into perspective.

I eventually learned why we were in Authie – other than the need to take stock of ourselves. Such information as percolated down to our lowly level informed us that we in VIII Corps were to line up with the left flank of the American Army in their all-out assault on St Lô and beyond. Their code name for the operation was Operation Cobra, while our contribution was code-named Operation Bluecoat,[2] which in the end was to take us to the River Seine and partake in the 'Great Swan'.[3]

Operation Bluecoat was based on the belief that in the American area to the west of us, only weak German forces held the ground,[4] and that the

---

1 See Daglish, Ian, *Operation Bluecoat*, Pen & Sword Books, 2003, p. 23.
2 Ibid.
3 This was the name given to the mobile operations, taking us from Normandy to the borders of Germany.
4 Daglish, *Operation Bluecoat*, p. 23.

British, with their battles for Caen and Operations Epsom and Goodwood, had drawn the bulk of the German armour into the Caen bridgehead. XXX Corps were to lead the British attack, with VIII Corps protecting the right flank directed on Dampierre south-west of Caumont. As the battle progressed, however, VIII Corps took the lead.

Still in Authie on 26 July, the Troop was warned at 1100 hrs to prepare to move at 1600 hrs, although the reconnaissance party would leave earlier to prepare gun positions at Verson (9765), off the D675 astride the River Odon on the west side of Caen. It was a precautionary action because an enemy counter-attack was expected. In the event, we did not have to move. On 27 July, however, we moved to Putot-en-Bessin (9370) south of the Caen-Bayeux railway line to engage in a counter-attack, but our services were again not needed. On the night of 28/29 July we made a move to Berigny (7065), which entailed another one of our series of difficult marches. This one was a 21-mile journey east to west, cutting across the normal north-south lines of communication of XII and XXX Corps. That we managed it without serious incident says much for the logistical skills of the Staff.

Authie had been very beneficial to us all, not only for the respite to gather our wits again, but also for the relief of tension that builds up in prolonged action. It was to be some while before another chance came.

# Chapter 12

# Operation Bluecoat

—∿∿—

On the morning of 29 July, a gun position was surveyed in, north-west of Caumont (690609) close to Sallen and la Jamerie, the guns taking occupation at 1900 hrs. In addition to the sixty 25-pdr shells carried on board, a further 200 rpg were dumped and distributed. I now knew that we were to engage in a full-scale attack southwards from Caumont, as usual in support of 3 RTR, as part of a move by 29th Armoured Brigade. We spent the night mostly in last-minute preparations, so there was little opportunity for sleep or relaxation.

At dawn on Sunday the 30th, the Luftwaffe came over and disrupted 8th Rifle Brigade, but it did not prevent us from firing a divisional barrage on the enemy forces at 0655 hrs. The fighting up front intensified, with 3RTR being heavily engaged, and we were kept busy firing continuously at very short ranges. My concern, as always, was on the state of ammunition stocks, which were being depleted by the hour, and I was in constant liaison with the Battery Sergeant Major (Jock Forbes) whose job it was to oversee what used to be called the Wagon Lines in horse-drawn days, but now was where the Battery support vehicles were kept, including reserve ammunition stocks. In answer to my requests, he was kept busy sending up supplies of shells with caustic comments, such as 'What the hell are you doing with the stuff?' This comment was just one example of the bizarre humour of the British soldiers that helped to maintain sanity in the most trying conditions.

It was the usual frantic day, with every single man feverishly doing something or other – the guns had to be kept firing without pause. Nor had the immediate countryside been completely cleared of Germans who persisted in fighting fierce rearguard actions which we had to eliminate. It was a relief, therefore, to receive orders to move at 2040 hrs southwards across the D71 to Bieville (683568). 3 RTR and 8 RB stopped short of St Martin de Besaces, where there was heavy fighting, and took up positions at St Jean des Essartiers. We stayed at Bieville overnight, firing on targets and taking on DF tasks until 1400 hrs on the 31st when I moved the Troop to the vicinity of the D9/D13 at le Perron (664530), north-west of Dampierre. It was not a long stay because I had to move the guns again, at 2000 hrs, to a position (667512) close to St Martin des Besaces. These moves were made in response to determined German resistance.

We had been continuously engaged in firing on enemy positions for forty-eight hours, and, apart from the strain on the men, I was concerned about our stock of shells. Supplies from the Wagon Lines had temporarily dried up, but I knew that somewhere in the area there would be an ammunition column of the Royal Army Service Corps. I therefore sought permission to go and see if I could locate them. It was given, but on the strictest of understanding that if the Troop moved in the meantime, then some indication would be given as to their new whereabouts. I also made sure I had a working wireless set as I did not relish a repetition of the Goodwood fiasco.

I set off in the Bren carrier with the phlegmatic Driver Smith around 2330 hrs. I had no particular location in mind, but I reckoned that the lines of communication would be more or less over the same routes we had traversed. I was lucky, because I stumbled across a column no more than a mile back, and I remembered my Goodwood experience. It would probably be no use searching for someone bound for my Battery, so I merely went along the stationary column asking the corporals for their particular destination. I picked my man and said, 'Who's your customer?' or words to that effect. He replied, 'X Battery.' I said, 'That's me. I'll guide you there.' I winkled him out of the column and made it back to my Troop as quick as I could in case my ruse had been rumbled. The RASC driver was only too pleased to get rid of his load and scurry back to base, so I was able to give the guns a hundred rounds each. I reasoned at the time that whoever expected to be in receipt of those shells, their ultimate destination would be on the Germans, so it didn't matter who fired them. Unfortunately my guilty conscience told me otherwise and I did wonder if the deprived X Battery might have required them far more than us. But by then it was too late for remorse.

Our objective for the first day of August was south of the River Souleuvre around Le Beny Bocage. So began a few days and nights of confusion and extreme danger because we (29th Armoured Brigade) had penetrated so deep into enemy territory that we found ourselves more or

Don Troop, 'H' (HAC) Battery RHA. Photo taken just before the crossing of the Rhine, 1945. Captain Philip Kinnersley (Troop Commander) is centre, 2nd row, with Second Lieutenant Charles Coad (GPO) on his right. The irrepressible Lance Bombardier Muscoe is on the extreme right, still in his overalls. (*Author's private collection*)

The author (centre, wearing trench coat), with members of Don Troop's command section, posing with a family whose farmhouse was used as the Troop Command Post. Holland, Christmas 1944. (*Author's private collection*)

Don Troop's four Sextons and crews. Photograph taken at Landswehr, Germany in August 1945. The Divisional sign of the Black Bull on a yellow background can be seen on the nearest Sexton. (*Author's private collection*)

Captain Kinnersley (left, forefront) leaning on an enemy tank. (*Author's private collection*)

Part of 'H' Sub, Don Troop, posing nonchalantly in front of their Sexton. (*Author's private collection*)

Sergeant Hemsley (right) with
one of 'H' Sub's crew.
(*Author's private collection*)

Sergeant Blaber, Don Troop's
hard-working Signals Sergeant.
(*Author's private collection*)

Johnnie Bryant (right), Don Troop's dependable wireless operator. (*Author's private collection*)

Bill Davies (left) and companion enjoying the sun during building works. (*Author's private collection*)

A smart turnout at Heide, Germany, March 1946. (*Author's private collection*)

Guard duty at Echerneforde. (*Author's private collection*)

'Hellzapoppin', the American White halftrack, which was Don Troop's command vehicle throughout the campaign, 1944–5. (*Author's private collection*)

Old comrades' reunion, Armoury House, London, 1991. Left to right: John Edwards, Viv Jones, Ted Charples, Harold Fort, Philip Kinnersley, the author. (*Author's private collection*)

The author in 2004, celebrating the 60th anniversary of D-Day (6 June 1944). *(Author's private collection)*

less surrounded by powerful elements of German armour and infantry. I now know that, among others, the 10th SS Panzer (*Frundsberg*) Division was on its way towards us, as was the 9th SS Panzer (*Hohenstaufen*) Division, and their marching orders, as we subsequently discovered, were timed for 1525 hrs.

We began the day at 0946 hrs by firing at a target of enemy infantry and guns (673424)[1] that were on the move in Le Beny Bocage, enabling our Battery Commander, Major Smythe-Osborne, to enter that small township at 1200 hrs, from where he took on more targets. At 2100 hrs I was ordered to move the guns (to 640541) where we stayed the night. The Germans were roaming all around in the vicinity and we had to be on full alert all night to ward off any attacks. There was to be no rest. I had to move the guns again at 1000 hrs on the 2nd (to 668432) for a quick action lasting two hours, when, on orders, we moved to Le Desert (693386), taking up firing positions at 1300 hrs.

This position was to be one of the most (if not the most) precarious of positions we had occupied since Operations Epsom and Goodwood. We stayed the night there in some trepidation, deep in enemy territory, literally surrounded by roaming German tanks and infantry. Our divisional tanks were fighting a hard battle on the outskirts of Vire in which we were directly involved and some sort of verbal altercation took place there. The road was the boundary between the British and American forces, and the Americans claimed precedence. 11th Armoured were therefore denied entry into Vire and so headed south-east into the German rear. So it was that at 0600 hrs on the 3rd, new positions were reconnoitred (706362), but the guns remained where they were.

At 1025 hrs I was informed that enemy tanks were very close and my right section of 'E' and 'F' gun subsections were withdrawn from an indirect firing role to take up anti-tank positions, shortly to be joined in that role by both 'Charlie' and 'Don' Troops, such was the imminent danger. We also formed ourselves into some loose infantry sections, although what we were supposed to achieve is questionable since we had no infantry or anti-tank weapons. Moreover, a Sexton self-propelled gun is not

---

1 Although many map references occur from now on, I cannot always identify the position by name, as I do not have a copy of the maps used at that time. Ordnance Survey were excellent in producing maps, but the nature of their gridding does not always comply with the more modern maps. Usually, we would fire one round on a map reference and then see where the round actually landed. The maps also did not necessarily meet sheet by sheet and it was not easy to identify the gap between them. Map references are essential to gunners, as only by knowing the position of the guns and their targets can a line and range be calculated.

an ideal anti-tank weapon because of its limited traverse. Half of the gun teams crouched low below the sides of the Sextons, whilst the other half dismounted to take up observation positions on the ground, their role to give early warning of approaching tanks or marauding infantrymen. It was reported that enemy tanks were as near as 200 to 300 yards away, but the close country was such that we couldn't see them. The guns were loaded with armour-piercing shot, which was a solid lump of metal about the size of a large family loaf, but we were apprehensive. A Sexton was not built for a tank-to-tank battle and the odds would certainly be against us if we actually had to engage in such an affair.

The weather was hot and sunny, with a clear blue sky, and our gun position was in a part of Normandy that would have been idyllic in more peaceful times. The countryside undulated with both high and low crests. The whole was made up of small fields and copses, bounded by narrow lanes, on top of which were thick hedges, so emphasizing a tunnel-like effect, especially in cloudy weather. The quiet country roads were mostly no more than lanes in between fields. The road from north of Bourcy and Presles and on to Estry marked the crest line in front of us.

The high point on this crest was Point 218, from where it was 3 kilometres to Estry and 1 kilometre to Presles, places that were to play a significant part in the day's events. Our immediate gun position was in the home paddock of a small farm situated on the left of a narrow lane leading up to the high point of the crest. Further on, looking east, the ground gradually sloped away to the edge of a wood. A thick wood, or dense copse, was to our left front, and to our immediate front we overlooked a small pasture field.

During the first few hours the situation around us was critical, as we expected at any moment to be attacked by tanks, or infantry, or both, but it did not prevent us from engaging in some quick, but intense, shoots. At 1315 hrs, the Battery was ordered out of its anti-tank role, with the exception of the two right-hand guns that were facing up the lane towards Point 218. Minutes later, at 1325 hrs, the Battery Captain, Captain Peploe, located three Panzer Mk VI (Tiger) tanks nearby and engaged them with our guns firing high-explosive shells. Unfortunately, there was one casualty in this affray (Gunner Beardesley) who was wounded.

Around this time, the regimental despatch rider (DonR), came chugging down the lane towards us on his motorcycle – Heaven knows where he had been since his approach was directly from the enemy-held positions. He came to report that the lane seemed to be clear of the enemy (information that proved to be incorrect), but that he had spotted a burning Sexton belonging to some other unit beyond the crest in front of us, and he thought there were some wounded men lying out there. We decided that the Sexton belonged to the Leicester Yeomanry of the Guards Armoured Division, who were known to be somewhere out on our left flank.

For reasons that have always escaped both of us, Lieutenant John Alford and myself either volunteered, or were ordered, to investigate this situation, with a view to rendering some assistance to the wounded. The DonR dismounted his motorcycle and tagged along with us. In retrospect, it was a stupid thing for us to do as we were deep in enemy country and the German armour and infantry were literally everywhere around us. The sniping was endemic. The fact that the DonR had ridden along the crest and down the lane was no guarantee that the area was safe – as things turned out, it was distinctly unsafe.

John and I, armed only with our revolvers, and the DonR, huddling close together, cautiously edged our way up the lane to the crest, a distance of about 300 yards, keeping low in the lee of the earth banks. We arrived at the staggered crossroads at Point 218, with Estry to the left of us, and gingerly crossed over to the other side of the road from where we could see the ground sloping away to a wood. We paused to get our bearings and to locate the burning Sexton, which was about 200 yards away. We didn't think it was safe just to stride over the open field from our present position, knowing that the Germans could be watching us, so we moved a little to the left where a lane led down the side of the field. As we neared the burning Sexton we had to leave the lane at an agricultural access to the field, and then approach the still smouldering gun over the shortest possible distance, which we knew would be exposed to enemy view. This we did, but only for a few paces.

We were three abreast, shoulder to shoulder – I was in the middle, John on my left and the DonR on my right. Then I heard the crackle of a machine gun and the hissing and whistling of bullets. The DonR, close to my right shoulder, was hit in the head, killing him instantly. John and I instinctively jumped to our left towards the thick hedge (later reported to be impenetrable) that separated the field from the lane, and forced our way through it, landing in a heap at the foot of the earth bank. Breathlessly we took stock, relieved to discover that we had not been hit.

We cautiously peeped back through the thick hedge to see what we could do for the DonR, who lay crumpled and motionless. The machine gun continued firing, the bullets spraying all around us. We knew it was not possible to approach the body or to render any assistance to the burning Sexton. We managed to locate the position from which the machine gun was firing. It was at the edge of the wood, but there was nothing we could do about it as the Germans were out of revolver range.

The German machine gunner obviously knew the countryside and must have realized that the only way we could retreat was back along the lane to the crossroads. He therefore kept up a constant stream of bullets along the edge of the lane, the earth banks giving us sufficient cover. Even so, there was still the open agricultural access to cross and at this point we would be exposed to the machine gunner again. We bolted across separately, doubled up, with a hail of bullets swishing overhead. It was only when we reached the lane leading back to the guns that we felt comparatively safe. We had tried our best, but tragically it was at the expense of a despatch rider, who had been a brave volunteer. And that was only the beginning of the unfolding events.

About an hour after I had rejoined my guns, I was sent back up the lane again, on orders from the Battery Command Post, to Point 218 to act as a FOO and to locate the whereabouts of any enemy tanks. This time I went up in my Bren carrier with the phlegmatic Driver Smith, and a wireless operator, to keep me in radio contact with the Battery. As we approached the crossroads at Point 218, I halted about 50 yards short, which was fortunate, as almost immediately I found myself about a hundred yards away from four Mk V (Panther) tanks, probably belonging to the elite Panzer Lehr Division that was known to be in this area. There they stood to my right front, well camouflaged, on the edge of the copse, silent, sinister, brooding and threatening, their long-barrelled, high-velocity, 75mm guns laid at the horizontal. Oddly, there were no Germans in sight, so I presumed they were all aboard. These tanks must still have been there when John and I went up the lane previously and it was fortunate that we had missed them. It was also possible that they were the tanks that were expected to attack us earlier. What was to be done?

The tanks made no move and I presumed they had neither heard nor seen me. I asked Driver Smith to reverse as quietly as he could without unduly revving the engine, which he did and we stopped after about another 50 yards. I then went back on foot in the direction of Point 218 and radioed back what I could see. I did so with great trepidation because if the

Battery Commander, or the Colonel, ordered me to fire on them, I would have to give my own position as the target location, and I was not particularly enthusiastic about that. I was then ordered to stay where I was and to report events. The only way I could carry out these orders was to go back on foot to where I had first seen the tanks, taking with me a remote-control handset.

I spent half an hour or so observing, during which time there was no sign of movement by the enemy tanks. I was still very uneasy about this situation because if someone at the guns decided to take matters into their own hands, they would have to use my position as the target, in which case I could expect the imminent arrival of an unwelcome shower of high explosive, finishing me off once and for all. However, I had little time to reflect on this unwelcome scenario as I had to keep up a stream of commentary over the air back to my Regimental Commander, Colonel 'Bob'.

This uncomfortable situation was not improved when, to my consternation, I saw a group of German infantry coming up through the wood that lay on the right side of the lane, presumably to join up with the Panthers. Since their approach might lead directly past my position, it was time for me to go somewhere else. I made my way cautiously on foot back to the Bren carrier, tucked in at the side of the lane, and established wireless contact again with the Battery Command Post, which in turn reported back to Regimental Headquarters (RHQ). I described the situation as I saw it and to my considerable relief was instructed to return to the Battery; but this was easier said than done. Another group of German infantry emerged from the wood almost at my side and I realized that the only way back was to fight our way out. I therefore engaged them with the 0.30 Browning machine gun mounted on the Bren carrier and they returned fire, fortunately inaccurately. This action lasted only a few minutes, when to my surprise and relief the German infantry decided to clear off. I assisted them with a long burst from the Browning, which I believed to be of good effect.

In the resultant confusion of my firing at them, and they firing at me, Driver Smith was somehow able to back down the lane in reverse until we reached comparative safety. Back at the guns, we stayed there for the rest of the day, and had to fire DF tasks all through the night, many of which were dangerously close to our position, so that regretfully we had to decline some of those tasks. Then, in the midst of all this, further orders were received.

At 0200 hrs during the night of the 3rd/4th, I was doing my usual duty as Relief GPO, leaving Charles Coad to snatch some much-needed sleep, when the Battery CPO, Lieutenant Harold Fost, sent along the basic details of an artillery barrage that was to be fired at 0730 hrs on the 4th. My assistant was Gunner Offord, a Brighton policeman in civilian life, and both of us were tired out to the extent that it took an effort of will to remain awake. Gunner Offord seemed to be far more gone than I was.

Working out an artillery barrage is a complicated mathematical procedure and in our tired state, working in near darkness and in expectation of a surprise visit by the enemy, it was heavy going. Map references have to be plotted on a gridded Artillery Board, so that the range and bearing of the targets can be calculated accurately. An artillery barrage is a procedure whereby a line of shells begins on a pre-established Start Line, then creeps forward at, say, 50-yard intervals, so allowing the attacking infantry to move forward behind its cover. It is a delicate operation, as the lives of our own troops would be at stake if the barrage were incorrectly constructed. It seems that a company of the 2nd Warwicks were to mount an attack to clear the Germans off the high ground around Point 218, and the barrage was intended to support them.

Gunner Offord and I worked for four hours by the aid of a dim oil lamp, computing the minute detail for each gun. The slightest error could mean that shells intended to fall upon the enemy might fall on our own attacking troops. However, in spite of all the constraints, we were able to send the completed scheme to the Battery Command Post for checking at around 0630 hrs. At 0700 hrs, I awoke Charles Coad to get him ready to control the actual firing at 0730 hrs, but he said that as I had done all the work, I could do it. I alerted all four guns to stand by at 0715 hrs and made sure that they knew what they had to do. The 2nd Warwicks had moved on earlier through our position to the Start Line, and all was ready for 0730 hrs. At the appointed moment, I began the series of firing orders and the barrage continued for half an hour. It served its purpose without incident for the 2nd Warwicks gained their objective. I felt rather pleased about it all.

Later, at 1150 hrs, RHQ alerted us that enemy infantry were known to be only 500 yards away, although at that moment we were painfully aware that they were closer to us than that. We knew the position of several of them from my adventures the previous day, but a Panther Mk V was spotted (702934) close by. So once more we had to take up all-round anti-tank positions and deploy accordingly. John Alford was ordered to go back up the lane and he took with him my two right-hand guns, making contact with the enemy infantry (701386) and then engaging another tank (702386).

'D' Troop's GPO, Charles Coad, was then also ordered to go up the lane with the two remaining guns, leaving me in charge of what was left of the Troop. This meant that he needed another Bren carrier, as mine had to remain with me in case of further orders. He hadn't got very far up the lane when the same Germans (presumably) who had fired on me, ambushed him (693386). Fortunately, he was able to scramble out, escaping back to the gun position, but the driver and the Bren carrier were captured.[2] The four guns eventually returned to the gun position, but in the ensuing melee, Lance Sergeant Bennett was wounded.

About this time the Regimental Second in Command, Major Farquhar, visited us and ordered me to get one gun ready to go up the dreaded lane at 2200 hrs that evening. I had four guns from which to choose and we did this simply by the gun sergeants tossing a coin. It was dangerous to travel the lane in daylight, as events had proved, and we knew the area was infested with enemy infantry and tanks, but to do the same trip in darkness was a different matter. None of us relished the prospect. Fortunately, at 1600 hrs these orders were thankfully cancelled, and we moved out of this precarious position to one on the Presles ridge about a mile away to our right (695360), which the enemy had just vacated.

We arrived on this sinister ridge at dusk and began firing immediately at fairly short ranges. The four guns were sited along the front edge of a line of tall trees, with our sister 'C' Troop occupying a position about 300 yards to our rear. Their targets were further away than ours and so they were firing over our heads. The Germans, who had themselves occupied the same position only a couple of hours earlier, knew the range to a yard and were able to plaster the gun positions with shells and mortar fire. About ten o'clock in the evening, Gunner Weir, 'F' subsection's driver, who was the oldest man in the Troop, was mortally wounded in the back by a large shell splinter.

Attached to us was a section of 20mm light anti-aircraft Bofors guns, and it became necessary for them to engage enemy infantry only 200 yards to our rear. In leaving Le Desert for the Presles ridge, we had moved from the frying pan into the fire, as it were!

That night resembled a Wagnerian scene as the fearsome exchange of fire and counter-fire continued on to the next day, the 5th. Even so, as the

---

2 Gunner Morgan, the driver of the Bren carrier, was taken prisoner but later managed to escape on foot.

day wore on, the conflict became more intense, and at 1800 hrs, and again
at 1900 hrs, the Regiment of twenty-four guns fired forty rounds per gun
in unison (a thousand shells delivering 11 tons of high explosive). Enemy
shells and mortar bombs eventually made the gun position untenable and
at 0100 hrs we moved back to our old position at Le Desert, arriving at
0210 hrs; within minutes, at 0235 hrs, we had to fire some urgent SOS
tasks. Bad as this previous position had been, it was preferable to Presles.

Firing continued most of the day, 6 August, through most of the night
and on to the next day. (We had no idea that the same day the Germans
elsewhere at Mortain had launched a desperate counter-attack against the
Americans.) At 1805 hrs, our Troop Commander, up forward, found
himself firing a medium regiment of 5.5-inch guns, and at 2225 hrs, one of
our chaps crawled forward into the wood facing us, reporting seeing a Mk
VI Tiger tank a hundred yards ahead (722342). The next day was quieter
but things hotted up again on the 9th when, at 1120 hrs, we had to fire
several smoke screens, named Hen and Cock, increasing the rate of firing
to ward off counter-attacks. By this time the gunners were exhausted, as we
all were, almost to the point of stupefaction.

We stayed in this exposed position at Le Desert until the 11th, when we
took part in a major operation code-named Operation Grouse, mounted by
29th Armoured Brigade, in support of the Guards Armoured Division and
the 3rd Infantry Division. We fired two barrages in support of our
attacking infantry, following it up with a single heavy concentration. Heavy
bomber support had also been laid on, but for some reason was cancelled
so we took on those targets at a rapid rate of fire.

On 12 August, I had to lead the Troop twice to new positions (700343
and 722345), though I do not remember much about them, except we were
glad to get away from the position that had been one of great anxiety, and
to be mobile again. It was now Day 14 of Operation Bluecoat.

At 0800 hrs on the 13th, we moved across country over open fields and
came into action (726445), where we engaged in some desultory firing.[3]
Next day I moved the Troop at dawn and came into action almost
immediately, moving again at 1340 hrs (765405). It seemed to be becoming
a war of movement at last, which was our prime role. On the 15th, we
moved three times, once in the morning (745382), then in the afternoon

3 It was on this day that a young subaltern joined us. He was Patrik Delaforce who, in later years, wrote a
history of the 11th ('Black Bull') Armoured Division.

(780368) and lastly in the evening (793376, west of St Vigor-des-Mézerets), which improved the morale of the men quite considerably.

The 16th was also a day of movement, for we moved twice, once at 1006 hrs (819334), and again at 1542 hrs (866271). On the 17th, we moved three times, at 1111 hrs (937242), then at 1400 hrs (939245), and again at 1700 hrs (943245), where we were stonked by German 88mm guns, which was most unpleasant.

We reached St Honorine La Chardonne on the 18th, moving on to Taillebois, east of Athis, where we came into action (044221). We stayed there during the 19th until 1600 hrs, when we moved again (179217). Battery HQ took three prisoners from the German 635th Grenadier Regiment and not to be outdone, we took ten prisoners in pouring rain at 0700 hrs the next morning. We moved from there at 1500 hrs to Cui (220220), just outside Occagnes, north-west of Argentan on the N158.

It was a great relief to be on the move again. The Regiment was trained for mobile warfare and a static role, so efficiently done by the Field Artillery, was not entirely to our liking. Epsom and Goodwood, and the early part of Bluecoat, by the nature of things compelled us to adopt a field role, but we were eager to be up with the tanks again.

So after the beginning of our normal mobile role, we came into action close to the River Orne, or one of its tributaries, on the outskirts of a small town called Putanges (on the western edge of the 'Falaise Pocket'), close on the heels of the Germans who were fighting bitter rearguard actions, fragmented though they might be. We did not know it at the time, but 29th Armoured Brigade, among others, formed the southern anvil, as it were, of the Allies closing the Falaise Gap, thus trapping the German Seventh Army. 11th Armoured Division was busily engaged in fighting the retreating Germans, and at Putanges I saw some of them only 400 yards away on the edge of a small wood manning a *Nebelwerfer* mortar, pointing menacingly in our direction. The guns were in action on rising ground and there were no obstacles to the line of sight of the German mortar.

Our guns were engaged in firing at targets in support of 3 RTR, which meant that this task had to take precedence over everything else, so we had to accept the consequences of leaving the German gunners to get on with what they had in mind. I watched the German team loading the mortar, then retreating 15 yards or so, ready to fire it by remote control. It was pointed directly at us and I saw sheets of flame as it was fired. I then heard the terrifying screams of the sirens attached to the bombs as they descended around the gun position, exploding in bursts of flame and debris; miraculously no one was hurt, nor was there any damage to the guns. All I could do was continue watching, but having fired, the German crew scurried off, abandoning the mortar.

During a lull shortly afterwards I was approached by about a hundred of the town's inhabitants, who had taken shelter in a large barn that lay behind us on the other side of the road. I went across to talk to them and was able to assure them, in execrable French, that for them the war was over. For a few moments I was a local hero and showered with embraces.

Later on it was my turn to be on GPO duty all night, which was quiet and peaceful, and when I handed over to Charles Coad at about 0500 hrs I thought it would be prudent to spend my precious sleeping time in a shallow trench, which I dug. I was awakened shortly afterwards, only to find that I was covered from head to foot by crawling black beetles whose nest I had disturbed. Don Troop was then treated to the ludicrous sight of a naked sergeant major beating the hell out of his battledress and plunging into the ice-cold waters of the nearby stream.

On the 21st, we moved in pouring rain from this elevated position to Argentan, but because the Americans, coming up from the south, disputed the boundary between us, we had to halt for a time until there was an amicable settlement. We had stopped at the stables of a handsome stud farm for horses, recently overrun by the Americans, and the signs were there to see. At the gateway, a dead young German lay sprawled on the ground with a bullet in his head. The fine buildings beyond the driveway had been looted. Eventually, the order came to move on, and a route through Exemes and Croisilles was taken, passing through the Foret de Gouffern, before we came into action at Huliviere (496452) at 1400 hrs.

This route took us much closer to the rout of the Germans trapped in the Falaise Gap. The scenes we came across were quite indescribable. The roads, narrow at the best of times, were choked with debris – human, animal and material. Dead Germans lay in obscene positions; bodies on the road had been run over because there was not enough room for tanks or other vehicles to swerve round them. Other bodies were tangled up in wrecked guns, vehicles and tanks. The stench was sickening. Many enemy tanks, having run out of petrol, were abandoned, whilst others leaned at grotesque angles, some actually upside down. Fully serviceable guns had been tossed aside as if by some giant's hand and dead horses were everywhere. British and American fighter-bombers had done their deadly work well. We couldn't get through this carnage quick enough, but it was painfully slow going.

When we eventually came out of this scene of destruction, another problem presented itself – booby traps and mines. The Germans, wily as ever, had booby-trapped and mined anything that might hold up the pursuing forces. A small example will illustrate the point. We came to a settlement that was no more than a group of agricultural cottages, and halted for a few minutes. On our left the cottages stood back from the road, with small front gardens. On the ground by the side of one of the gate posts a portable typewriter in seemingly pristine condition glistened in the sunlight. We were sufficiently wary not to investigate further and moved on, however, as one of the guns passed by, someone threw something at it and the typewriter exploded, demolishing the gate and part of the garden wall. If anyone had succumbed to the temptation it offered, they would probably have been blown to pieces.

After leaving Huliviere, and having passed through the dreadful scenes described above, we arrived at 1930 hrs at a gun position (541407) which also became the temporary location of 29th Armoured Brigade's Tactical HQ, so we were in very good company indeed. The next day we moved off to fire from another gun position (583404), arriving at 1130 hrs, and at 1700 hrs, after it had rained all day, we finally came out of action at Aube-sur-Rile, west of L'Aigle.

It was now three weeks since we had arrived at Le Desert – twenty-two days and nights of constant fighting, mostly at very close quarters. As far as we were concerned it was the end of Operation Bluecoat, especially as our role was now taken over by the Guards Armoured Division, so leaving us free for fresh tasks. We now had a few days out of the line. It rained all night of the 23rd/24th, and all day on the 24th, but the weather cleared up on the 25th, making for a hot and sunny day.

# Chapter 13

# Amiens

—⚬—

Our reward for sixty-six days in close contact with the enemy came at last – we were now having five days out of the line at Aube-sur-Rile. An orgy of gun, vehicle and personal maintenance was undertaken, and we refuelled, rearmed and rested. Hot baths had been rigged up in which we indulged ourselves. Cookhouses were installed, and good old ENSA came along and put on daily concerts and cinema shows. A dance was held in the Town Hall and all the young ladies turned out. Unfortunately they all seemed to be accompanied by their mothers, which rather put a dampener on some of the men's expectations. Even so, flowers, fruit and wine were showered upon us. We even got paid. There was, however, an underlying feeling of sadness as we learned that the three major battles of Operations Epsom, Goodwood and Bluecoat had so far cost 11th Armoured Division 4,000 casualties – about a third of its full complement. It was small consolation that we had taken 3,000 prisoners.

Our past, mostly Field role changed at this juncture, as 11th Armoured reverted to its original formation, comprising the 29th Armoured and 159 Infantry Brigades. The 50th and 43rd Infantry Divisions had relieved us, allowing us this period to refit. Our task now, as part of XXX Corps, commanded by the legendary Lieutenant General Sir Brian Horrocks, was to give close support to the tanks when the offensive resumed, against the Seventh German Army which was hurrying back to whatever positions it might seek to make a stand. 29th Armoured Brigade, with 3 RTR and 'H' Battery, was to lead as usual, being a situation we relished, as it gave us a feeling of superiority!

All good things come to an end, however, and the five days out of action quickly passed. In pouring rain, on 28 August,[1] we moved off at 1000 hrs with 3 RTR to an area at Champenard a few miles west of Vernon on the

---

1 Jean Brisset, in *The Charge of the Black Bull*, puts the date at the 27th.

D316, arriving at 1600 hrs. During our five-day sojourn at Aube, the 43rd Wessex Division had forced a crossing on the 26th over the River Seine at Vernon, north of Paris (Operation Neptune), and a pontoon bridge had been built as the RAF had destroyed the massive road bridge. I viewed the pontoon replacement with great trepidation – the Seine is very wide at this point (approximately 215 yards), with a high water level – and led the guns to the west bank at 1800 hrs, just as the sky was darkening.

I watched closely as tank by tank negotiated the pontoon bridge, a procedure that did nothing to increase my confidence. A pontoon bridge is no more that a series of flat sheets laid transversely over a series of pontoons laid side by side.[2] As it is a floating structure, secured to the banks at both ends, it is not, in my untutored opinion, a particularly stable arrangement. Thus, as the tanks went over, they appeared to wobble from side to side and we wondered if their tracks were submerged below the lapping surface of the river. If ever a jar of rum was needed, now was the time.[3] No such luck, however. On the west bank, engineers and military police were in command, signalling each tank over at the appropriate moment. The richness and extent of their vocabulary was to be admired, but they did a marvellous job.

Then it was our turn and the sky was getting darker. In front of me was an American White half-track, which served as the Troop Gun Command Post, with the GPO (Charles Coad) in charge. 3 RTR had gone on ahead, and we were behind the tanks of the Fife and Forfar Yeomanry and the 23rd Hussars. I was behind the GPO in my Bren carrier (known as TLD). As this was a lightweight vehicle of some 4 tons, compared to the 32-ton Shermans of the tank regiments,[4] it meant that, as they cockled on the pontoon, they caused the Bren carrier to wobble even more.

The Seine stretched away each side, with a width of over 200 yards, and it looked most forbidding with its strong flowing current. The sky darkened by the minute, which did not improve driving conditions. The drivers' eyes were glued to the narrow line of the pontoon, knuckles glowing white as their hands tightly gripped the steering tillers. Some drivers later reported cramp from their feet arching sensitively over accelerators and clutches. Neither was the way forward made any easier by the wash thrown up by the vehicles in front. The first few yards were not too bad, but then, as the

2 A pontoon is a floating, hollow metal or wood structure, supporting a roadway over a river.
3 In the First World War a 'rum issue' was available to the men before they went 'over the top'.
4 32 tons compared to 4 tons. The White Half-track weighed 8.5 tons.

pontoons sagged under the weight of the tanks, water sloshed over the tracks so that the roadway in front temporarily disappeared from view. It was a nightmare drive and it was with huge relief that we found ourselves safely on dry land on the opposite bank of the river at Vernonnet, a small, pleasant riverside settlement, now completely deserted.

By now the night was pitch black and, with all the action and tension of the past few hours dissolving into slight relief, we then found ourselves entirely alone. No other units were in sight or sound. I bunched the guns nose to tail, forming up in the little square of Vernonnet. My job was to see that every one had crossed over safely, so it was with considerable relief that I was able to report to the GPO that all was well. Then the worry began to nag again as our detachment from the rest of the convoy produced an unreal situation. There were no inhabitants or anyone else to be seen and we began to feel lost. The tank regiments had gone ahead and there seemed to be no other units behind us. It was strangely quiet and somewhat sinister. Because of the way we supported the tanks, each troop was normally attached to a particular squadron, so it was that 'Don' Troop, of four Sextons, one half-track and a Bren carrier, was alone, with no unit to which we could attach ourselves. There was certainly no one to the rear because I doubt that any tracked vehicle could manage that pontoon in the pitch darkness.

Charles and I conferred and decided to move off very slowly out of the square, into the dark night, nose to tail, with Charles in the lead, and me immediately behind 'nursing' the guns. We crossed over a railway line and stopped a few yards further on at a 'T' junction. The ground on the other side of the junction rose steeply in front of us to a high spur, so the road out of the village could only go right or left, curving round the base of the spur in a 'U' shape. The road to the left led north-west to Tilly, and the road to the right led south-east to Gasny and Giverny. Beyond the escarpment lay the huge dense Foret de Vernon, criss-crossed with rides and tracks that provided excellent cover for any German forces likely to appear from the direction of Beauvais. The close topography was also amenable to Free French Resistance Fighters (FFI).

We paused at the 'T' junction, wondering whether to go right or left. There was no one around to whom we could ask directions. Charles Coad and I conferred again. There were no signs to give us a clue. We studied the road surface to see if there were any helpful track marks, but it was too dark to come to any convincing conclusion. We elected, therefore, to go right for no obvious reason. This road, curving anti-clockwise, led steeply upwards in the valley created by two adjoining high spurs, and, not for the first time, we ran into an enemy ambush.

German infantry suddenly spilled over on to both sides of the road in front of us. Fortunately the curvature of the road, together with the dense darkness of the night, meant that the most they could see was Charles's half-track and my Bren carrier; the guns to our rear were out of sight. They were probably doubtful of what might be behind our two vehicles and this no doubt caused their tardiness in attacking us with random bursts of small-arms fire.

In the midst of this affray, Charles dismounted and ran back to the guns, yelling to the sergeants to turn the Sextons round in the road, whilst I stayed with the Bren carrier firing the 0.30 Browning machine gun at no obvious target – but it made a comforting noise. It seemed to be a miracle that the Sextons all managed to face themselves in the opposite direction in a matter of minutes, considering the road was barely a two-lane carriageway. The night air was filled with the noise of the screaming engines at full revolutions, which was a good thing, because it obviously confused the enemy barring our way. Charles quickly returned to his half-track, but both he and I were now at the rear of the guns. The driver of the leading Sexton wisely stayed where he was until we re-established ourselves at the front of the column; in any case, he had no idea where he might be going. Somehow, we managed to get back to the front to resume the lead, leaving the enemy to their own devices. This time we took what was the left road out of the 'T' junction, leading to Tilly.

This time the road curved clockwise and, like the other road, it ran through a valley, rising to meet the plateau at the top of the spurs. Again we had only moved a short distance along the road when Charles's driver brought the half-track to an immediate shuddering stop, the guns behind frantically trying not to ram the Sexton in front. The reason for this emergency stop was that Charles found himself looking straight down the muzzle of a long-barrelled gun of a huge tank that almost blocked the road.[5] I could see two of the tank's crew up in the turret, and they were indisputably Germans. There was absolutely nothing we could do about this extraordinary situation – it seemed as if our war had now come to an end.

For a few moments, nothing happened. We just remained where we were, waiting for something, or someone, to make a move. Then Charles dismounted from the half-track and I followed suit. We stood at the front of

---

5  This was either a Mark V or a Mark VI, a 60-ton Tiger tank that mounted an 88mm gun.

the tank, staring up at the two Germans leaning out of the turret, expecting them to do something. I think Charles and I had the same feeling that if we gave ourselves up, it might persuade the Germans not to fire. But before we could do anything else there was some sort of commotion to our right on the high earth bank lining the road. Jumping down onto the road, some unrecognisable and somewhat disreputable figures appeared shouting and gesticulating. They said they were '*Les Forces Francaises de l'Interieur*' (FFI), and they had just disabled this tank by lobbing a grenade or two into the open turret from the top of the bank as it passed them by. They were beside themselves with their success and we were, of course, immensely relieved. When we asked about the tank crew one of the FFI climbed onto the tank and yanked out two very dead Germans. Neither had any legs – gruesome, to say the least, and we didn't enquire further about the rest of the crew.

The FFI were jubilant over their success and, producing from nowhere a bottle of wine, asked us to join in. We shared a bottle (or two), whilst the gunners brewed up some tea. The FFI confirmed that our tanks had recently passed this way, but we could find no explanation as to how the enemy tank had managed to appear between our own tanks and us. However, we now felt that if we continued on our way, we might catch up with 3 RTR. Then, as it so happened, our wireless sets came to life. We had hitherto had to maintain wireless silence until ordered otherwise. Charles put on his earphones, trying to sort out speech from the crackles, and someone in an irate voice enquired, 'Where the hell are you?' He thought it prudent not to answer for the time being.

After about half an hour, during which we learned a little of what was happening nearby, we set off, leaving the FFI to see if they could do something about those who had ambushed us. We cautiously approached the edge of the plateau at the top of the hill and saw flames coming from a large barn to our right, lighting up the night sky. We passed it by carefully and proceeded towards the next village. This was Tilly and we were then suddenly called into action (473776), which meant an immediate dash into the nearest suitable open space off the road. Unfortunately, this happened to be only 200 or 300 yards in front of the burning barn, not a comfortable position to be in because we were silhouetted against the glare of the conflagration, and therefore showing ourselves up as easy targets for any snipers that might still be around. Fortunately, as the night wore on, the flames began to abate.

This gun position, imposed upon us without any previous

reconnaissance or preview, was off the road, and bounded on its right by a low post and wire fence, behind which was a thick wood. I controlled some shooting during the night, having persuaded Charles to nod off for a while. We were firing in response to 3 RTR, with whom we had re-established contact, as they were engaging pockets of resistance. This activity kept us on the go all through the night, making rest difficult for the gunners.

It was my usual night duty and as dawn came slowly through on 29 August, I was alarmed to see about thirty Germans coming out of the wood a few yards away to our right. We would normally have been an easy conquest in this situation, for we had few small arms with which to defend ourselves. To my relief, however, they had their hands up, apparently happy to surrender. They had already disarmed themselves and despite language difficulties I discovered that they were the self-same infantry who had ambushed us back in Vernonnet. They had lain up in the wood all night, waiting for the dawn to offer surrender. Some of my chaps were keen to strip them of any useful possessions and I had a tough job stopping them. That they would be stripped of their personal possessions later on by others was not in doubt, but I made sure it wouldn't be by us.

It is difficult to reason why I acted like that. This enemy company, by their own admission, had not only ambushed us coming out of Vernonnet but had also set the barn alight. They were therefore the same men who, a few hours ago, were intent on killing us. Now they were our prisoners. We had no means of dealing with them, for we had no food or water to give them and no one spare to guard them. Should we have relieved them of all their possessions? Clearly, they were the views of many of my men, but I stopped them, with reluctant compliance. There was no thought in my head of the Geneva Convention, or any altruistic ideas – I just couldn't bring myself to loot a defenceless party. They were a bedraggled, miserable lot, ill dressed and obviously hungry. They were quite unlike what one imagined a fanatical German soldier to be. In a sense, one could feel sorry for them, so my mixed emotions turned to anger, and, pointing to the rear, I told them to 'Geraderaus, schnell', leaving someone else deal with them.[6]

---

6 'Geraderaus, schnell', meaning, I hoped, 'go straight on quickly'. There was a not dissimilar dilemma faced by the Germans, but with a more dealy outcome, at what became known as the 'Malmedy Massacre'. Some 160 Americans were taken prisoner by Colonel Peiper's SS men in the little Belgian village of Baugnez in the Ardennes Offensive in December 1944 (usually referred to as the 'Battle of the Bulge'). These prisoners were an embarrasment to the German tank crews and so were lined up and shot, killing 142 (see Wilmot, Chester, The Struggles for Europe, The Reprint Society, 1954, p. 652). There is a more detailed account in Whiting, Charles, Jochem Peiper, Leo Cooper, 1986, pp. 59-67. He puts the number of murders at eighty. Peiper was assassinated in 1976.

It poured with rain all day, not stopping for twenty-four hours. Nevertheless, it was a day of movement and great activity. We began shooting at 0700 hrs (target 507820), switching at 1000 hrs to other targets (area 548940). At 1015 hrs I had to move the Troop to another position (5158340), and again at 1200 hrs (534874). We stayed in position, engaging targets until 1530 hrs when we moved again. At 1900 hrs I led the guns to another position (589986) where we spent a very wet night. It had been a hectic day of constant movement and firing, but what we didn't know was that this day began for us a vital part of the 'Great Swan'. This was the long-expected breakout from the Seine bridgehead, and we covered 21 miles in nine hours during the day, notwithstanding that we came into action four times. Even so, General Horrocks thought this effort was not good enough because the Germans were capable of quick recovery, and it was vital that the bridges over the River Somme at Amiens be captured before that happened.

During this long slog, our Battery Commander, Major Smythe-Osbourne, acquired a proliferation of enemy targets, and directed on to them the fire of a medium regiment of 5.5-inch guns firing 100-lb shells. While this was going on, the Troop was by no means idle, as already described. The following day, under low clouds and threatening weather, at 0900 hrs we fired heavily at retreating infantry, which went on all morning. We moved again around midday and came into action at 1337 hrs (699131), firing on a bearing of 30 degrees. At 1715 hrs, in pouring rain, we came into another position (881257) – and that began another interesting episode.

This location was not particularly inviting, being not so much an action position as a laager for the night. It lay just off the road to the right and seemed to be no more than a clearing in a wooded area, but it was large enough to accommodate 'A' Squadron of 3 RTR and us ('H' Battery). We were soon joined by a divisional supply column from which we drew petrol, ammunition and food. We were fortunate in that respect as we were short of such necessities, and some units to our rear had to be grounded for lack of them. The weather was bad, with heavy bursts of rain, but it gave us a short respite to take stock of things after the previous hectic days and nights.

Somewhere behind us, Lieutenant General Sir Brian Horrocks, Commander of XXX Corps, and Major General 'Pip' Roberts, our Divisional Commander, met at 1615 hrs, to discuss 11th Armoured

Division making a night march to Amiens to seize the bridges over the River Somme before the enemy had time to blow them up. This was a particularly hard matter to contemplate because the tank and Sexton drivers, who had been driving for thirty-six hours without a break, were exhausted, but there was no hesitation, despite the usual empty British grumbles.

It was clearly going to be a risky venture, but it did not deter 'Pip' Roberts from accepting the challenge, especially as General Horrocks assured him that he had laid on a full moon for the night, an expression that has since passed into legend. General Horrocks, in *Corps Commander*, Sidgwick & Jackson, 1977, wrote that 'only a first-class, well-trained Division, with a very high morale, could have carried out that night's advance.'

There was no moon, of course. The clouds were thick and low, it was pitch dark, the drenching rain intensified, and no one had any idea where the enemy were, or in what strength – but we had the orders, and that was it. We set off around 2200 hrs, following behind 3 RTR. They had a system, I believe, whereby whoever was appointed Orderly Officer for the day automatically took the leading tank. If this was true, a young subaltern must have led this most difficult night march. It was an eventful night with drivers falling asleep at the tillers at each halt. These were frequent and at times, fantastic as it may seem, there were actually enemy vehicles and tanks joining our column, mistaking us in the dark for their own.

We did not know where the enemy lurked, so the armoured column tended at first to proceed cautiously, nose to tail, but in the knowledge that there was a high element of urgency in the task, knowing that we had to be at the bridges at or before dawn on the 31st. Although we therefore speeded up a little, there were frequent halts, some to get our bearings and others because we came up against enemy resistance.

Whoever was leading was doing a wonderful job of map reading. The distance we had to cover was estimated to be some 40 miles, which meant that we had to do around 7 miles an hour to reach the Amiens bridges on time. The tanks in front, when approaching a village or settlement, assumed they held Germans, and so the column tended to by-pass each one, simply by going off the road and ploughing across country on compass bearings, so increasing the length and the intrinsic difficulties of such a venture. When we had no alternative to entering a village, all the inhabitants turned out in the dark, rain-swept night, many in their night clothes, and showered us with flowers, food and wine, wildly happy to be liberated.

This night march was a most hazardous thing to accomplish because one never knew what lay ahead or on our flanks. There was an entertaining interlude on one such occasion. We bumped our way over fields in the dark, through copses and orchards, bypassing German-held villages. The very wet night seemed to become darker and visibility (without vehicle lights, of course) was poor to nil. As we gained firm ground back on the road, the drivers, with true British grit, often chose to occupy the left-hand side of the road, ignoring the continental system. All of a sudden, we were surprised to see a motorized column of German infantry coming towards us, going by with barely a yard between the passing columns. The Germans were apparently very angry that we did not observe the rules of the road and dire insults were traded between the parties. Hostilities remained verbal, however, not physical. One could not speculate where they thought they were going, but it was certainly not in the direction of Germany!

This hilarious incident was not quite at an end, however. A few minutes later we came to a halt and were astonished to see a German military policeman, immaculately dressed, directing traffic at a crossroads. It was even crazier when he held up a group of German vehicles to let us pass. It seemed that he was there to control traffic, and, in his stoical German manner, did so, impervious as to its nationality. Some wag in our column even handed him a bottle of wine! To cap it all, there was a diversion as the German tanks, which had tagged along behind us, believing the column to be theirs, had to be winkled out.

As the march continued, it was not without incident. There were some accidents and some breakdowns, with the weary drivers having difficulty in keeping awake. Other British troops joined our column and it took some time to sort things out, but we eventually came to the outskirts of Amiens as dawn was breaking. At 0600 hrs on the 31st, the tanks captured the railway bridge intact and half an hour later the main road bridge over the Somme. We took up what was for the time being a precarious gun position at 0530 hrs (064356), which was alongside the riverbank at the foot of one of the bridges – and there I got into a little bit of trouble.

There were a number of German lorries parked in the field that had been hastily abandoned and we quickly explored them for anything that might be useful. I came to one loaded with German greatcoats. These were new and ankle length, made of good material, and were a distinct improvement on the one I possessed. I tried one on and someone handed me a German scuttle helmet. I was very pleased at this pantomime and paraded up and down in what I believed to be true Teutonic fashion, with a poor imitation of goose-stepping and the outstretched arm. A shot rang out during this ridiculous performance and a bullet whizzed close by. I ducked behind one of the lorries – to be confronted by a grinning Tommy in a scout car who had apparently entered into the spirit of the carnival. What ensued is not repeatable – suffice to say that I allowed the war to continue without the benefit of any further Thespian entertainment on my part.

At half past five in the morning of the 31st, while I was recovering from the embarrassment of the incident, we took two prisoners who were willing to give us valuable information about the enemy's whereabouts. By 0705 hrs, 3 RTR, with us behind, had penetrated 800 yards into Amiens, where we encountered some enemy transport. They were quickly sent packing.

The next few hours were hectic. The enemy was in the process of withdrawing and there were many columns of motor transport to be dealt with. The two talkative prisoners also informed us that there were about 4,000 German troops in Amiens. At about 0730 hrs we engaged four Mk III or Mk IV tanks on a ridge, scoring hits. By 1300 hrs the Citadel in the town was ours and the enemy faded away very quickly.

A few hours later, two other bridges were captured intact.[7] We stayed in this position, or close by, until late afternoon, during which time our guns were in constant action, taking on enemy tanks, motor transport and infantry. Another unit also captured a column of infantry as they marched their way to breakfast, and an irate General Eberbach, Commander of the German Seventh Army, dressed only in his pyjamas, had his own breakfast rudely interrupted by British tanks that he believed to be 30 miles away. In the afternoon, more of the FFI came out in the open and although they were a ruthless lot, they were of great assistance in locating targets and guiding us around the town. We moved to another position at 1715 hrs (116606), from where we fired on a number of opportunity targets. By nightfall on 31 August, Amiens was in Allied hands.

---

7 The three bridges in question were code-named Faith, Hope and Charity.

117

*Chapter 14*

# Antwerp

—⚡—

lthough 11th Armoured Division was now firmly established in Amiens, General Horrocks was determined to push on north of the Somme. The Division spearheaded the advance and, where it met with opposition, assisted the infantry in returning fire before moving on. We closely followed on behind 29th Armoured Brigade.

In the evening of the 31st, therefore, units of 50th Division arrived to take over Amiens, and at 0630 hrs on 1 September we set off for Antwerp, travelling over the open rolling plains familiar to soldiers of the First World War. The enemy resistance was still evident, however, and at 1705 hrs we had to go into action (370088), firing on a bearing of 30 degrees. This firing continued until well after 1900 hrs.

This was the beginning of the race to the Rhine and the next few days, as General Horrocks wrote in *Corps Commander,* 'were the most exhilarating of my military career'. We moved fast along a centre line, with little opposition, on a route that took in some important crossroads (104595), thence to Rainville (1416), Rubemore (1771), Thierres (2383), Mandicourt, Couturelle (2691), Somerin (2695), Avesnes (2999), Tilloy (3205) and Aubigny (3407).

At many of these places, the people turned out in droves to welcome us as liberators, showering us with gifts of wine, flowers and embraces. This headlong rush was brought to a halt, however, at 0730 hrs on 1 September when we came into action (370088), firing on a zero line of 30 degrees. Our FOO was kept very busy and we continued firing for most of the night. Even so, the leading units of 29th Armoured Brigade were able to reach Arras by nightfall.

We moved off at 0755 hrs on the 2nd, following closely behind 3 RTR, and it is worth repeating at this point that we had become an integral part of the tank regiment, so absorbed were we in all their contacts with the enemy. Our Battery Commander, Major Smythe-Osbourne, in his

Sherman tank was literally glued to the side of the Regimental Tank Commander, Lieutenant Colonel Silvertop, to enable him to bring our guns into action at a moment's notice. Inevitably, on long marches like this, the wear and tear on the tracks of the tanks and self-propelled guns took their toll and Charlie Troop had to leave two guns behind due to mechanical faults, although Don Troop suffered little on that account. Our route was through Servin (3713), Bouvigny (4014), Aix (4315), Grenay (4517), Loos (4918), Hulluch (5122) and Wingles (5323). Progress that day was slow as we met opposition all the way at points where enemy anti-tank guns held up the tank column for a while.

It was at Wingles that disaster struck. We arrived there at some time late in the morning, the town appearing to be an outer industrial suburb of Lille, and halted on a residential road lined with terraced houses built right up to the back of the pavement. The tanks at the front of the column were dealing with a pocket of resistance and there was nothing we could do to render any assistance, constrained as we were by the dense ribbon of residential development.

I dismounted from my Bren carrier to chat with the Command Post chaps riding in the half-track in front of me, and stood at the tailboard exchanging words with Sergeant Sharples who was sitting on the offside facing Gunner Baun, the gun fitter, who was sitting on the nearside. Around us were the welcoming inhabitants eager to show their gratitude. Up front, we could hear some of the action taking place as the leading tanks came under fire, when suddenly there was the swishing sound of an approaching missile. This turned out to be a solid armour-piercing round coming from an enemy anti-tank gun. Before we could take any cover, the round hit the wall of a house on the opposite side of the road just a few yards in front of us, before ricocheting in our direction.

All this happened in the fraction of a second. The round (similar to the size of a family loaf, but ten times heavier), deflected by its contact with the wall, ripped through the canvas cover of the half-track, passed closely between my head and Sharples's shoulder, and hit Gunner Baun full in the chest. The weight and speed of the round propelled Baun bodily out of the half-track, throwing him through the canvas cover and across the pavement, where his lifeless body crashed into the wall of a house. He was killed instantly. Charles Coad jabbed morphine into his body but nothing could be done. His chest was caved in and his tongue swelled so much that it forced his mouth wide open into a grotesque shape.

Ted Sharples and I were considerably shaken, not only because of Baun's unexpected, one-in-a-million death, but also because we knew that the round had missed our heads by only a few inches. Had it deviated a foot or so in its 2,000-yard trajectory, either Sharples or myself would have been instantly decapitated. This realization of near death was upon us as we applied ourselves to dealing with the unfortunate Gunner William Baun.[1] The local people, who had scattered for shelter, quickly recovered their alarm and gathered round the dead man. Then down came the order from up front: 'Prepare to move'. What was to be done? We couldn't take the body with us and we couldn't bring ourselves to leave him where he fell. The locals came to our assistance, however, and took charge of the dead man, so resolving this dilemma. We learned later that they gave him a Christian burial in the local cemetery.

War is the history of such events and we had to go along with it. I felt his death as keenly as most, for he was one of my four-man crew in the Bren carrier (Driver Smith, Gunner Baun, Lance Bombardier Muscoe, the vehicle fitter, and myself). Normally, Baun would have travelled with me, but on this occasion he elected to ride with his friends in the half-track. One cannot foretell such matters.

The column moved forward in a sombre mood, allayed only by coming into action at 1310 hrs (584197). The afternoon period gave us a respite, put to good use by gun and vehicle maintenance, with some attention to one's person. But it was a short break for, at 2100 hrs, I had to move the Sextons to another gun position (576208) to enable us to close up with 3 RTR who were preparing to move off the next morning. Even so, we were all on the alert, for we learned from another self-propelled unit (86th Field Regiment RA) that twenty enemy tanks and 300 infantry were advancing close by to blow up a bridge (559193), although as far as we were concerned nothing came of it.

Nothing is certain in war, as in life. While we were preparing for an early morning move, it was interrupted before dawn on 3 September, at 0455 hrs, by enemy mortars firing in our direction (561257), and we had to take evasive action and managed to get away at 0730 hrs to begin another march forward. This time the route took us to Maurchin (5722), Provin (5823), Annoclin (5925) and Allennes (6126), although not without incident. At 0900 hrs we went into action (615260) to shoot up three anti-tank guns and

---

1 He was the man in Operation Goodwood who, on his own and completely unarmed, took the surrender of seventy-four German infantrymen from the 716th Infantry Division.

about a hundred enemy infantry. I was also warned by the FFI that German infantry and tanks were approaching us from the rear along the self-same route. This was more believable than the previous similar warning because we could see the leading German vehicle some distance behind us, but someone must have engaged them, for we saw no more of them. I also heard, at 0940 hrs, that the enemy still held the small township of Seclin that was on our route.

This place brought back memories of 1939/40, when I was a gun sergeant with 10th Field Regiment RA. It was in this area that we spent the nine months from September 1939 to May 1940 (the 'Phoney War' period), and where we fought a bitter rearguard action later in May. Sergeant Moran ('G' subsection) was particularly moved by us being there. He had spent the whole of those nine months in Seclin, and was anxious for us to make a detour, if we could, to look up a family who had befriended him. I had to remind him gently that there was still a war on and that we weren't on a 'Tour of the Battlefields'.

At 1007 hrs we came across four enemy gun pits, lately occupied by German self-propelled guns, which had been engaged in firing at us. We examined these abandoned pits most carefully in case they were booby-trapped, but the most prominent feature was the smell. For some reason the Germans and their equipment had a peculiar smell that we came to know quite well. It was sickly and unpleasant, and we never knew its precise nature. The nearest guess was that it was the ersatz gun grease that they used, but we were not certain. Then we had to take on two enemy self-propelled assault guns (Sturmgeschulz) at 666254, but we found them to have been abandoned by their crews.

Immediately afterwards, at 1010 hrs on the 3rd, we moved off and drove into Seclin (6727) as it had been liberated only a few minutes earlier. It was a 'lucky' event and although Moran couldn't locate his friends from the past), we found crates of champagne reserved for the Wehrmacht. We quickly changed its destination and four very happy gun teams continued the advance. It was fortunate that there were no breathalysers around in those days – Charles Coad and I were particularly worried because had we met up with any Germans at that time, it would probably have been dealt with more by hilarity than by hostility!

At 0230 hrs on the 4th, we came into Erembodigem in Belgium (shades of 1940), where we stayed for a couple of hours, moving off at 0530 hrs, and passed through Templemars (6829), Vendeville (7029), Lesquin

(7331), Ascq (7633), Chereng (7933), Sin Crossroads (814330), Willems (80235), Touflers (809388), Festingue (826388), Nechin (8430), Estambourg (8740) and Pecq (8941).[2] It was at this last place that a strange event occurred.

Pecq seemed to me to be a small town on the Franco–Belgium border. We were running short of fuel and our armoured column accordingly halted right on the border itself to refuel from trucks of the Royal Army Service Corps (RASC) loaded with 4-gallon petrol containers. They must have been following closely on our heels to come up in so short a time. Petrol tanks were quickly refilled and some ammunition replenishment also took place. These are the two main features of warfare that gave me the most concern, even taking precedence over food. Sustenance may be gathered en route, but petrol and ammunition are not necessarily indigenous commodities.

All this took place in a matter of half an hour before restarting the advance. All, that is, except 'F'subsection, commanded by Sergeant Charlie Musker whose Sexton refused to move. As Acting Troop Leader, I investigated the problem, which seemed to be either a clutch failure or a gear malfunction. Either way, the Sexton remained obstinately motionless. Lance Bombardier Muscoe, being the first line of vehicle maintenance, raced out of my carrier, hopeful to put matters right, and though we all had great faith in his mechanical wizardry, it was to no avail. His small toolbox, overflowing as it was, remained unequal to the task. The next line in the matter of mechanical failures was the Light Aid Detachment (LAD). This was a 3-ton truck forming part of Regimental HQ, which travelled at the rear of the column to see to events of this nature, manned by experts from the Royal Electrical and Mechanical Engineers (REME). Alas, their roadside repair skills also did nothing to get the machine moving. The third line on which to rely for help was to await the arrival of a larger unit of REME, which had workshop facilities, but that meant that I had to abandon 'F' subsection to its fate. What with two guns from Charlie Troop out of commission, the Battery was down from eight guns to five, and we were to lose one more later on.

This delay meant that Don Troop was well behind the tanks it was required to support and I had a job to get the remaining three guns up to rejoin the column. It is as well to note the date of 'F' subsection's

---

2 The reader may find the naming of these routes to be shade tedious, but it serves to record what could be forgotten. As these places were newly liberated, we were suitably rewarded by the usual gifts.

breakdown, namely 4 September, because it was ten or eleven weeks before we saw the crew again – minus the Sexton.

What happened after we moved off without them has always remained somewhat vague. What little I learned later was that immediately after the breakdown our centre line of advance was abandoned in favour of some other route, with the result that everyone behind us changed direction, so that the expected arrival of REME at 'F' subsection did not take place. Indeed, as the story goes, 'F' subsection saw little or nothing of the British Army for weeks on end, marooned in a small town in which there seemed to be no military presence. They could not abandon the motionless Sexton (no gunner ever abandons his gun), so they stayed put. For the next few weeks they were fed and watered by the local inhabitants, with Sergeant Musker hoping that someone somewhere would locate them. Eventually, they were found, I think, by a French unit and handed over to REME at Tournai. The Sexton presumably was towed away and the crew finished up at a series of replacement camps in Belgium. They rejoined us in Holland in November without a Sexton, ten weeks after the event, looking somewhat crestfallen.

Whilst on the subject of breakdowns, an unusual night was spent by a gun subsection in our sister 'I' Battery, commanded by Sergeant O'Malley, a smallish, bright Scotsman, with twinkling eyes and humorous manner. The story goes that their Sexton lost a rubber bogie that supported the tracks. This was not a particularly serious matter as the Troop's vehicle mechanic, with the crew's support, replaced it in a couple of hours, by which time the column had moved on. The night was dark when they restarted and, coming to the outskirts of a village, they drove through it, not knowing that the column had by-passed it because of a warning that some Germans were there. Sergeant O'Malley was unaware of this information, but was suitably apprehensive to take certain precautions. After the repair to the tracks he thought it prudent to take shelter in a small commercial garage to decide on their next move.

When they peeped out from the closed-up garage to take stock of the situation, they were surprised, to say the least, to see a German sentry pacing up and down in front of them. They were not to know at that time that they had chosen to take shelter next to a house used as a German post. How they were not detected is a mystery, as one cannot back a 23-ton Sexton into a small building without someone noticing it. It was generally supposed that the Germans mistook it in the dark for one of their own. But there they were, holed up, guarded by an unsuspecting German sentry.

They spent an anxious night, wondering what to do, gradually working out a plan. The idea was that just before dawn, whilst still dark, they would ram a shell up the breech and start the engine at the same time. They would then charge through the closed door and make their escape. This is easier said than done. A Sexton engine needs a few minutes running time to bring the oil pressure up to a certain point, otherwise damage can occur. Furthermore, not only is it necessary to ram the shell into the breech, but a brass cartridge case also needs to be inserted behind it. It is not a quiet operation. They decided to take a chance and do all the actions at once – it worked!

The Sexton was put into first gear, the clutch let out and they charged out, with the garage door torn off its hinges, still clinging to the Sexton. They pulled sharply to the left and roared through the village street, much to the surprise and consternation of an early morning patrol of sleepy Germans on their way to breakfast. Fortunately, they soon met up with us and all was well. No doubt the crew have dined out on that event for the last sixty years.[3]

Returning to the narrative, we had moved off again at 0530 hrs, joining the main Brussels-Antwerp highway at Impde (590695), having passed through Leuvenstraat (423642) south-east of Alost, Boukout (4463) north of Hekelgem, then east to Assche-Ter-Heyden (4863), Buda (505638), Road Junction (490675) at Droeshout, then east to Merchten (5368), Road Junction (582670) at Wolverthem, turning north to Meusgem (579678), then moving cross-country to Impde. From there we drove north to Londerzeel (5972), north to Neerhavert (5875) and De Wolf (591781) at Driehoecke, then to Rijweg Crossroads (620788) west of Willebroeck, and north-east to Boom (6482).[4]

The march had, however, taken its toll in breakdowns, because instead of having eight guns between 'C' and 'D' Troops, we were down to four 'runners and shooters', having lost another gun somewhere, so we had to form ourselves into a composite Troop. There were also more dramas awaiting us during this eventful day of 4 September.

The first of these concerned the indefatigable Lance Bombardier Muscoe and myself. At 0730 hrs we came into action just off the main

---

3 This story has become apocryphal through embellishments, but is founded on fact. O'Malley drove into a village where the Germans were moving out, and hid until their final departure.
4 This route can be found on the original map sheets, both numbered 8, supplied to me by Captain Harold Fost.

road at Hoeksken (617778) south-west of Willebroeck, to cover the crossing of the Rivers Rupel/Nethe at Boom. We were being machined-gunned at the same time from somewhere on our right front and whilst the tanks dealt with this matter, I saw, about 200 yards up the dual carriageway an apparently abandoned German car on the opposite side. Muscoe and I decided to investigate. It was a smart Opel tourer, painted in appalling camouflage colours, and was probably a staff car judging by it contents, which included bags of real tea. We decided to appropriate the car, with the idea of using it as Muscoe's maintenance vehicle, thereby removing his overflowing impedimenta from my carrier. As I drove the Opel back to where our guns were, just as I was getting up speed and passing our guns on the left, the bonnet blew open and up, obliterating my view of the road. Muscoe dealt with this in his imperturbable manner and I turned the car round by driving over the central reservation and headed towards the guns.

Almost immediately we were showered with machine-gun bullets. Muscoe was in the passenger seat on my right and bullets passed between us smashing the instrument panel and the windscreen. The firing continued and one bullet severed the gear lever just below my hand, with other bullets shredding the tyres. Even so, I managed to drive it to the rear of the guns, where we dived for cover.

To our embarrassment, a British scout car drove up, commanded by an irate corporal, who enquired in no uncertain terms, 'What the hell were you up to?' It seemed that he saw this German car coming towards him, which then turned around ostensibly to escape, so he shot it up. He appeared to be not all concerned that we were British and still alive. As far as his marksmanship was concerned he would have preferred to see us dead! Neither was our Battery Commander well pleased with our purloining the car, as he had spotted it too and had earmarked it for his own purposes; now it was a total wreck – the second time a British scout car had taken a dislike to me.

The second incident also occurred in the same position. The guns were still on the road, tentatively laying off at 45 degrees, pointing towards where the enemy was thought to be, when a small group of ragged men appeared out of a nearby ditch. They were Belgians and they told us that just along the road there was a concentration camp – would we liberate it? This was the infamous Fort Breendonck camp for political prisoners. We couldn't do it as we were still in action positions, but a couple of Shermans from 3 RTR moved in and did the job. (Years later, I visited the camp. It has been kept as a museum exactly as it was and even thirty years on it was horrifying to see the conditions in which the prisoners had been kept, and to see the hanging scaffold and the posts to which they were tied before being shot.)

The third incident was more exciting in its own way. It seems that a certain Belgian Engineer Officer, Lieutenant Robert Vekemans, was directly instrumental in enabling 11th Armoured Division to enter Antwerp more easily than expected.[5] He had reconnoitred the bridges over the Rivers Rupel and Nethe, and observed the preparations the Germans were making for blowing them. He therefore persuaded 3 RTR, with us following, to strike north from Alost and follow the southern winding banks of the River Rupel to Willebroek where we turned left at the crossroads leading into Boom. We arrived short of the Pont van Enschodt, and actually saw Vekemans threatening a German NCO with a revolver, before cutting leads that would have blown up the viaduct.

The column then drove pell-mell into Antwerp itself, amidst cheering crowds. At 1300 hrs on the 4th we came into action (653886) and our Battery Commander was the third of the leading tanks to enter the city. A quarter of an hour later we had to fire a smoke screen for some reason or other, but by 1400 hrs the situation devolved into a matter of confused fighting and celebrations which went on for the rest of the day and night. The Battery Commander enjoyed himself by attempting to tour the city with a small group of tanks from 3 RTR, meeting up twice with groups of Germans, but the welcoming crowds and the narrowness of the streets, together with patriots climbing onto the tanks, curtailed his ambitions somewhat.

The next day, saw us still stationary in the city. We had been ordered to halt as we were outstripping our administrative resources, which still came by lorry from the beachhead some 300 miles back. Petrol was running short and some historians allege that we halted from exhaustion, but that was not so. Tired out though we were, the adrenaline was still flowing from the remarkable achievement of capturing Antwerp and the docks intact (less the Scheldt Estuary). We did some desultory shooting first thing in the morning, controlled by an officer at Hoboken, continuing until 0700 hrs on the 6th, when the situation intensified.

During this time, however, I was able to detach myself from the guns

---

5 For a fuller account of this, see Moulton, J.L., *Battle for Antwerp*, Ian Allan Publishing Ltd., 1978, p. 22.

and make a trip on foot into the city centre in the company of Regimental Sergeant Major Reynolds. Cheering crowds surrounded us and pressed champagne, ice cream and flowers on us, with women climbing all over nearby stationary tanks. We were accosted by a man who said he was the manager of the city's leading department store and would we allow him the honour of a visit, where anything we fancied would be ours for the asking. We accepted the invitation and looked around, meeting the staff who followed us around like sheep. I chose a penknife and RSM Reynolds chose a wallet – *both of which we paid for in Belgian francs!*

After leaving the store with much goodwill, we were approached by a lady of a certain age, who, speaking English with a northern accent, invited us to her house. She was apparently the English wife of a Belgian electrical contractor and had managed to live out the war unmolested, although that her teenage son, who was a gifted musician, had been conscripted into a German orchestra to entertain the troops. She showed us where they concealed the wireless set that kept them in touch with the BBC. It was encased in one of the settee's feet, with the aerial wound around inside the back of the settee. She gave us English tea from a carefully hoarded store.

In the evening of the 5th, the guns were still at action stations shooting up pockets of enemy soldiers, but the firing was such that we could manage with half gun teams. This enabled three men per gun to move off for a while, then returning to allow the other three the same facility. Both parties took advantage of the city's hospitality.

At 1900 hrs the next day, the 6th, we went into action on the edge of Central Park; across the road behind us was a modern block of flats. There, in the midst of our guns firing into the harbour, the hospitality of the Antwerp people was really appreciated when, later in the evening, the residents allowed us the use of their bathrooms for hot baths. It is difficult to describe the sheer luxury of being able to strip off a soiled and smelly battledress and soak in hot soapy water (we provided the soap). The wily chaps of the Battery Command Post even established themselves in a part of the flats.

The evening was also an interesting time because, whilst working on the principle of half gun teams, I was able to wander off on my own. I went along the road that bordered the Park, heading towards the city centre, where I came to a fork in the road formed by the extensive showrooms of the Ford Motor Company. On one corner was a café, already filled with our men having a whale of a good time.

I joined in and after a while a lady, apparently the owner of the cafe, beckoned me to come and join her. Not unnaturally this raised ribald shouts from the assembled company and some of them slanderously alleged that this sort of thing was always expected of me. Undaunted by these dire allegations I followed her out of the back of the café into the garden, where she handed me a spade and asked me to dig. About two feet down I struck a metal box which turned out to be a small, old-fashioned, tin cabin trunk, inside of which were a dozen or so bottles. She said they contained some very old cognac and she had been determined to keep them away from the Germans. They had been buried for over four years. I was ceremoniously presented with a bottle while the guzzling gunners maintained their suspicions, enquiring if I had taken payment in kind. I am somewhat ashamed to say that Charles Coad and I drank the bottle of precious liquid at one sitting later in the night, suffering for it the next morning!

All good things come to an end, however, and at 0730 hrs on the 7th we left Central Park with the objective of forcing a crossing over the Albert Canal. General Horrocks bemoaned the loss of the four vital days from 4 to 7 September. I did not know what was happening at the time because I had the idea that we were bound north-eastwards for Appledoorn, to enable an approach to be made on the Ruhr (we had actually been issued with maps to that effect).

Indeed, we certainly moved off to the north-east, but were then diverted south-eastwards. This drastic change of direction originated in the divergence of opinion between Field Marshal Montgomery and General Eisenhower – the former wanted to strike at Germany with a single thrust, whilst the latter wished to attack Germany on a broad front. The latter prevailed.

*Chapter 15*

# Holland

—∿∿—

A ntwerp was the end of the operation so far and seemed to me to be the end of the 'Great Swan'. From now on, the fighting was to become a case of attrition rather than that of movement. By this time we had covered some 580 miles from Caumont, inclusive of 340 miles covered in the past six days, fighting almost every day. Both the tanks and the Sextons had travelled that distance on their own tracks, without the aid of transporters – a record that might still stand today. Of the past six days in question, the Division had inflicted a great deal of punishment on the enemy, but we were fortunate in that our casualties were light in comparison. As the Division's historian notes: 'But any kind of military action, no matter how one-sided, involves calling a halt, making a plan, however quick and simple, giving orders, and some measure of deployment; and all this holds up the advancing column.'[1] He goes on, underlying a feature mentioned repeatedly in this narrative, that the strain on gun and tank crews, by covering prodigious distances, keeping in contact with the enemy and fighting to erase pockets of fierce resistance, without rest, was enormous. He observed that they had obtained just one night's sleep in a week, and that a short one.

As already described, we left Antwerp at 0730 hrs on 7 September, with the intention of forcing a crossing over the Albert Canal, thence to s'Hertogenbosch in Holland. We thus moved south-eastwards in the direction of the Canal, where 29th Armoured Brigade had orders to protect XXX Corps' southern boundary. We travelled the long distance to Deurne in bad weather, without any hold-ups, finally going into action in a flat, desolate and miserable landscape south of the village, where the 8th Rifle Brigade had run into some German anti-tank guns that had knocked out one Bren carrier and killed the crew. Their recently dug shallow graves

---

1 Palamountain, E.R., *Taurus Pursuant*, privately published, 1945, p. 57.

were by the roadside. I was leading the Troop at this time, apprehensive that the enemy anti-tank gun that had destroyed the infantry carrier was still active. I had to take a chance, but fortunately the Germans had abandoned their exposed position on my left flank, presumably aware that if they fired on us it would mean certain destruction for them. I then drove on for a short while, but had to turn back because of the fierce nature of the defenders. At 1100 hrs, I received orders to occupy the same gun position we had recently left.

Much to our discomfort, we stayed in this position until late morning on the 9th while the rest of the Division caught up with us, before moving again at 1200 hrs. The weather was again unkind to us, being wet, gloomy and cold. Here, because we were attached to 3 RTR, we were transferred from 29th Armoured Division to 159th Infantry Brigade.

In the many gun positions we occupied during the whole campaign, Deurne stands out as being environmentally the least hospitable. Someone in the rear, however, must have thought the same, because on the evening of the 8th, who should turn up but the Army Cinematograph Unit. They took over the village hall (a wooden structure), and put on a film that we attended on a half-crew basis. I think I even remember the film, featuring Nigel Patrick and Sheila Sims. The Germans, however, spoiled it for us somewhat by sending over a few shells which burst quite near, rocking the hut, the projector and the screen, and keeping us on our toes.

We evacuated this miserable position on the morning of the 9th, side-stepping a few hundred yards towards Pael, presumably by going south to Blankelaer, then north-east in the direction of Beeringen, where a new bridge had been constructed over the Albert Canal, which had now been crossed, and stayed there overnight until 0600 hrs on the 10th. We were still a composite Troop having lost several guns for one reason or another, but the two Troops, 'C' and 'D', were reformed, each with three guns. We then drove north-eastwards towards Peer along a tortuous route to just short of Helchteren (342745), in between some shooting on Kumsel only a mile beyond Helchteren. Later, at 2000 hrs, we moved into Helchteren itself, ousting a fragmented German Parachute Battalion. After an overnight stay, we moved to a fresh position at 1145 hrs and carried out some desultory shooting.

It was here that I took possession of a replacement Sexton for the missing 'F' subsection, which had been left behind at Pecq, noting that since their absence I only had three guns to care for. When the replacement Sexton arrived, I was quite convinced that it had been plucked from some scrap heap in the rear, for it was in a deplorable condition. My first impression was to send it back to whoever had the effrontery to send up such an object, but the exigencies of the moment prevailed. Some wag somewhere had christened it 'Cockney Kid', and that just about summed it up.

This Sexton was in an appalling state. I drove it round and round the gun position to see how it ran, putting it through its paces, and was not impressed. Worse still, there were no gun history sheets to record what the gun had done. Was it a new barrel, or was it clapped out (more than likely)? No one knew and we couldn't find out, having lost our gun fitter, William Baun in Wingles). The important point about this is that guns have to fire in parallel, unless programmed otherwise, and that guns should fire at exactly the same range as each other, and in the same direction. Without the gun history sheets, Cockney Kid could be sending a shell anywhere, and we couldn't let that happen as the lives of our own troops were at stake. Neither was there any time for proper calibration so we had to proceed by trial and error. Fortunately, we were able to promote Bombardier Syd Lyall to Gun Sergeant and between us we assembled a scratch gun team. Sergeant Lyall made an excellent job of quickly producing an efficient complement to the Troop.

At 1145 hrs on 11 September, the weather improved and the morning was clear and bright. Although 29th Armoured Brigade spent the day resting and reorganizing, we moved north and east to Peer (401821), where we fired intensively.

I hardly ever knew what we were firing at. Targets came by the dozen, and we responded quickly and efficiently. If only we had been given a little more information about the targets we were engaging, it would have given us a greater measure of encouragement, particularly when the gunners were dog-tired – and even more so when some indication would have been welcome on the success or otherwise of our shooting. Occasionally our action orders might begin: 'Take Post. Target Tanks'. But what sort? How many? What were they up to? We rarely knew. There is an indefinable sense lurking between firing at tanks and firing on exposed infantry, and gun crews tend to react accordingly, without prejudicing their orders.

At 1700 hrs on the 11th, I had to move the guns off again, this time north to Petit Brogel (398877), to await a fresh task. When I received the order to prepare to move, the new location that came over the crackling wireless net could only be deciphered as 'Betty Grable'. If the ordered location was 'Betty Grable', there could be nothing unusual about that. I accepted it as being a code name for somewhere about which we did not want the Germans to know. I perused the fragmentary codebook and conferred with Charles, but we could find no reference to Betty Grable. That particular lady was at that time a Hollywood film actress famous for her legs, who became an American pin-up girl. I had no objection to taking the Troop along to see her! No such luck, of course, but it did mean that someone had to be despatched to higher authority for clarification. Naturally, all was revealed (if the expression can be pardoned, dear Miss Grable), and it seemed that for once the new gun position was sent out in clear as Petit Brogel; we simply misheard it.

At Petit Brogel, the gun position was in the home paddock of a small farm. I lined up the guns about a hundred yards beyond, and parallel to, a farm track, on the other side of which were the farm buildings, laid out in the usual quadrangle style, with one side of the square left open. The centre of this three-sided arrangement was a cobbled yard, in which was the inevitable midden. When standing on the track with one's back to the guns, and facing the farm buildings, the right-hand side was occupied by the farmhouse itself, next to which and joined to it was a large barn containing bales of hay and a recumbent cow. With one's back to the farm track, the frontal view was to the rear side of the square, comprising the dairy, adjoining which was an archway that led into the fields beyond.

We were now apparently no longer under command of XXX Corps, but had been transferred to VIII Corps, and did not know at the time that we were not to take a direct part in the forthcoming Operation Market Garden, which was to be an airborne (Operation Market) and ground (Operation Garden) attack, to seize the area Nunspeet-Arnhem. 11th Armoured was to look after the right wing, if called upon to do so.

For once, there were no fire orders, and it was felt that for one night at least we might be able to relax a little. I therefore devised a sentry rota, while the rest of the headquarter section of the Troop found somewhere reasonably comfortable, in relative terms, to bed down. The Command Post team, of which I was a peripatetic member, chose the hay barn, and on conclusion of my duties around midnight, I joined them there. Naturally, all the best places had been taken. The only place left on which I could stretch out was up against the barn door, the bottom edge of which was a foot or so short of the ground. This place was also close to the recumbent cow. Even so, I spread out my makeshift bedding, and, for the

132

first time for a long period, I divested myself of my trousers, folding them up to form a pillow, and tucked my revolver by the side.

I hadn't slept much over the past few days but although I was tired out and exhausted, sleep did not come. An hour or so later I heard footsteps rattling on the cobbled yard. Because the barn door did not reach the ground, my view was no more than at ground level. It was a bright moonlit night and all I could see from my prone position were a number of legs encased in jackboots. It did not take a genius to realize that the occupants of these boots were Germans. What was more disturbing was that the boots also accommodated stick grenades stuffed into the uppers. It only required one of those grenades to be tossed into the barn and that would be the end of the war for half a dozen of us.

This unwelcome party of German soldiery seemed to be somewhat agitated. I froze solid, my mind racing, at the same time being painfully aware I was clad only in my khaki shirt. The marauders passed by, barely a yard from my face, and I reckoned there were about a dozen of them. They hammered on the door of the farmer's cottage adjoining the barn. The old farmer, awakened from his bed, stood in the doorway, dressed in a voluminous nightshirt, trembling uncontrollably. The Germans demanded food and the old man, frightened out of his wits, was only able to stutter that the English were here. The Germans did not wish to stay to consider the situation and not knowing precisely where the English might be, scattered for a moment like headless chickens. This brief respite enabled me to gather some of my senses, for I was sensitive to the fact that any one of them could quickly end the proceedings by the employment of a grenade or two, although they wouldn't have got away with it.

I managed to straighten up, deeply aware that I was naked from the loins down. I fumbled around for my revolver, but the recumbent cow, now awake and attempting an upright position, impeded my efforts. After a frenzied moment, I managed to retrieve it and pushed open the barn door, emerging into the courtyard just in time to see the enemy disappearing in a great hurry round the corner of the building. They fled along the farm track at high speed. I must have appeared to them to be some weird apparition, silhouetted against the moon, with shirt tails flapping around bare legs. I ran after them, firing all six rounds in my revolver. I never knew if I hit anyone but they all escaped except one man who ran off in a different direction and fell into the arms of a bemused sentry holding a Bren gun that he had no idea how to fire.

This farce did not end there because the Battery Commander, who had heard the commotion, grabbed the field telephone lying by his camp bed to enquire what all the fuss was about. At the same time, anxious to do something else, I went to my Bren carrier that was nearby, on which was mounted a 0.30 Browning machine gun. I did not know if there were other Germans swanning about in the area, but if there were, then I ought to be ready for them. I started the engine, still *sans pantalons*, and swung the carrier around. In doing so, I ran over the telephone cables lying on the ground, and the steel tracks snatched up and entangled the wires. This pulled the telephone away from the BC's hands, and he was forced to follow it on his hands and knees to maintain contact. I stopped the carrier and dismounted. There we were together, he in his pyjamas and me in my shirt. The gunners seemed to be highly entertained by this pantomime, but studiously tried to look elsewhere, knowing that the Battery Commander had a very short fuse.

It seems that the fleeing Germans were part of the Hermann Göring Parachute Division, a fanatical body of men who, it is said, would rather be shot than surrender. They had been forced out of Helchteren, away to our rear, and were trying to escape to their own lines, such as they were.

After this incident, which did not appear to the Regimental Colonel to be amusing, we came to know Petit Brogel quite well as we stayed there for almost a week. There was plenty of shooting to do, as Market Garden activated many of enemy units. The clearance of most of the enemy from the area between the Albert and Meuse-Escaut Canals, allowed us to spend this welcome period in Petit Brogel for rest and maintenance. Even so, because of local raids by the Germans on some of the villages, we were kept busy from time to time.

The reason for this unaccustomed stay out of the mainstream of events was our exclusion from Market Garden.[2] We had led the British Army all the way from Caumont, but now the Guard's Armoured Division had taken over, so at 1200 hrs on 16 September we formally came under command of VIII Corps. Nevertheless, we gave some peripheral support and on the 18th we engaged targets from gun positions at Ellicum (4683) in support of the King's Shropshire Light Infantry, and on the 19th at Caulille (465900). I learned from someone that the fresh 107th Panzer Brigade had arrived at Venlo station from the Eastern Front, and that we could expect more trouble.

---

2 The airborne assault to gain the bridges over the Waal-Maas and the Rhine.

This latter position at Caulille seemed to me to be a somewhat sinister place. The weather had turned gloomy again and we came into action in a field that was bounded on our front by a thick line of trees. I had the instinctive feeling that the wood, only 200 to 300 yards away, was held by the enemy; if so, we were only 400 yards or so apart. What was scary was that Ted Sharples, the GPO's Assistant, had to go towards the wood by a hundred yards or so in front of the guns with a director,[3] to survey in the guns. On a good day, this can take about four minutes. For reasons I cannot remember, I decided to accompany him, maybe because we shared the same fears. During those few minutes we both felt we were being watched by enemy eyes. The feeling of being a sitting target became so strong that we hurried through the survey and raced back to the guns. I can still recall the mental picture of Ted running as fast as he could over the rough field, with the director still attached to its flapping tripod, trying desperately not to trip up. Our fears seemed to be groundless, or, at least, if there were Germans there they kept quiet. We were just tensed up, that was all, and we carried out some shoots without any interference. Even so, we spent the 19th still in the same position, but no one relaxed.

At 0600 hrs on the 20th, we left Caulille, but had to move back to Petit Brogel as we could not travel off the roads due to the unsuitable terrain. We came into action at St Hubert (4394), then moved north to the crossroads on the Hamond road, and east to Hamond (4797), where we crossed the Dutch border at 1300 hrs. Map reading was not easy as the Ordnance sheets issued to us did not correlate to each other.

At 1715 hrs I was ordered to move the guns out of Hamond to take up a position south-west of Leende at Liender Stryp (448076), where we stayed overnight. At 0900 hrs on the 21st, I led the guns in the direction of Eindhoven and we had to take up a position at 497103 just north of Heeze, firing on a line of 45 degrees against enemy resistance at Lierorp, south-east of Eindhoven. At 1155 hrs we moved north to Geldrop (469160), where the line of fire swung round to 20 degrees. By 1758 hrs we had moved to a place immediately north-east of Eindhoven (477198), in sight of the Wihelmina Canal, the Dommel and the Willens Canals. The American 101st Airborne Division had captured the town, and enemy resistance was persistent and fierce. On one occasion we were ordered to fire upon the modern Phillips Electronic factory campus that was being used by the Germans as an observation post. This was a single gun-

---

3 A form of theodolite used to survey in the guns by reference to a map and the direction of fire.

pinpoint shoot at an upper-floor window at fairly short range and we cheered every burst, an amusement not likely to be shared by the factory owners.

Although we stayed there overnight, we were continuously in action, and this intensified onwards from 0630 hrs on the 22nd, when we fired on the main bridge over the canal that was held by two platoons of German Engineers. All were either killed or wounded and eighteen prisoners were taken. (This time we did know what we were shooting at!) This rate of fire went on until 1140 hrs, when we were firing almost into Helmond (554221), and by 1315 hrs we were supporting 3 RTR who were held up at the river by bazooka and machine-gun fire. We entered Helmond at 1400 hrs and stayed there firing until 1730 hrs. Resistance came mainly from the riverbank where the Germans held a small chateau-like building with Spandau machine guns. I was up front with the Troop Commander's tank, sheltering by a corner of a building overlooking the river, and was both surprised and alarmed to note that the Spandau bullets were capable of penetrating the Sherman's turret armour by an inch or more.

Our sharp shooting, as displayed at the Phillips factory, was repeated at 1730 hrs when we engaged a fortified house just south of the railway line south of the town, scoring three direct hits. At 1800 hrs, I shifted our position marginally to Hoog Geldrop (483164), firing on a zero line of 45 degrees.

In the early hours of the next morning, the 23rd, we moved off once more, taking a tortuous dog-leg route south and eastwards, with many halts, arriving at Someren (589123) at 0630 hrs. We established a gun position within the village, being surprised and delighted to find nearby a Co-op shop still open and trading. Some of us joined the queue of villagers waiting to be served, and by paying real Dutch money,[4] we stocked up mostly on bread and butter, neither of which ever seemed to come our way in the rations.[5]

At 1100 hrs, whilst this orgy of shopping continued, we fired on a zero line of 20 degrees at targets in and around Liesel (646154), one of which was a Mk III German tank. As often happens in this form of mobile warfare, the Liesel targets had to be engaged at a fairly long range

---

4 The local bank, by opening on time, further extended this bizarre situation, where we were able to exchange French and Belgian money for Dutch guilders – and all this in the midst of a battle!

5 Although bread as baked by the Army Catering Corps was freely available in the back areas, we did not get any until the end of September, some four months after landing on the beaches.

compared to our normal short-range firing. However, we returned to our normal practice at 1215 hrs, taking on a target west of Klein Heltrak (610101) at a range of not more than 1,500 yards, the target being some transport in an open field (652135). This continued until 1605 hrs, when we fired into an enemy group of about fifty infantrymen. Liesel still continued to be a place of firm resistance, especially at about 1815 hrs when we fired a very heavy concentration from at least eight guns. Eventually, at 1900 hrs on the 23rd, we reached the edge of Liesel. The night of 23/24 September was still uncomfortably noisy and I was relieved to move us away at 0600 hrs the next morning.

The advance continued at 0730 hrs and we approached Asten (615141), north-east of Zomeren (or Someren), where we came under heavy shelling and mortaring, Gunner Wells being wounded for the second time by an 88mm airburst. North of the village, a small river or stream crossed the road, which had a bridge over it. There had obviously been a hard fight there by the Herefords because I had not seen so many dead German and British soldiers in one place since Epsom and Goodwood. They were all grouped around the bridge. Some were still alive but badly wounded and a lone, brave and unknown Dutch girl in her teens was seen tending to them, friend and foe, as best she could. There was nothing we could do to help, except to give up some spare personal first-aid kits which we normally carried on our person.

The Troop was kept active all day, firing at a multiplicity of targets, but at 1600 hrs in the afternoon of the 24th I moved the guns north to Vlierden (624178), and immediately resumed firing on a zero line of 30 degrees in the direction of Deurne (not to be confused with the other Deurne referred to earlier), then lengthening the range to Milheeze (650215). At 1000 hrs the next morning, the Command Post personnel reconnoitred a new position north of Deurne just short of the target we had been engaging, but fresh orders came down and we went instead to Milheeze (648243), shooting on a line due north at 360 degrees. At four o'clock that day we reverted to the support of 3 RTR. We had literally been shooting in all directions, which gives an indication of the disorganized complexity of a mobile battle.

Later in the day, at 2000 hrs, we shifted northwards to Oploo in what was, in comparative terms, a considerable distance in one move, and I brought the guns into action (7163670), firing due east. This was a nasty and precarious position as we were being heavily shelled. The enemy appeared to be all around us and we were warned to be ready to defend ourselves. 'C' Troop faced east and my own 'D' Troop faced west; the enemy were said to be only 400 yards away. To the north and south of us there were some units who could protect us, but to the east and west the flanks were wide open. The guns were loaded ready, with the range set at 400 yards.

During this uneasy time, in the midst of enemy territory, our FOOs had established themselves in the village of St Anthonis, north-west of Oploo. At a crossroads in the village, an 'Orders' Group ('O' Group) took place, attended by the Brigade Commander, his Brigade Major and two colonels. At that moment, two German half-track vehicles came roaring down one of the roads, having been flushed out by the 15th/19th Hussars. The Germans fired on the group, wounding the first two named and killing the two colonels. One of these was Lieutenant Colonel David Silvertop who commanded 3 RTR. All who knew and fought with him felt his loss keenly. He was a Western Desert veteran and was one of the finest of tank commanders. It was of little satisfaction to us all that the Germans responsible for his death were hunted down and destroyed.

We spent an anxious night (25th/26th) at Oploo, compounded by bad weather, and we had to be fully alert, during which neither sleep nor rest was possible. Normally, I spent a fair amount of time throughout the night walking round the guns in the dark, checking on sentries, listening to the grumbles of the gun sergeants, who always wanted more of everything, and collecting data for entry into each of the gun history sheets, but not so tonight. Everyone was so gun-happy, I wouldn't have lasted ten yards!

Dawn on the 26th came as a relief of tension of the night, but to no one's surprise. At 0945 hrs, we were told to prepare for tanks, as a column was spotted moving north-west. This diversion was in the midst of a flurry of firing on targets from 1000 hrs onwards. In return, we were shelled by the Germans, and for a while the gun position was a maelstrom of bursting shells, interposed by our own firing. We suffered casualties, namely Gunners Scott and Tyson, who were badly wounded by shellfire. We were apparently supporting a unit, probably Engineers, who were constructing a bridge over a canal to allow the tanks to pass through. Our rate of firing continued all day until 1800 hrs, by when the guns had been in action continuously for over eight hours, firing thousands of shells. During all this time the targets were so concentrated that the guns' alignment remained only a few degrees each side of a centre line sector of 100 degrees. Even when we moved the next day, we fired very heavily at 1200 hrs on the same zero line.

The 28th was particularly bad as we suffered several casualties. In the evening we fired continuously from 2220 hrs until 0130 hrs. The 29th and 30th were just as busy, the latter being somewhat interesting. At 1030 hrs, an enemy observation post was destroyed. Then at 1600 hrs we took part in a massive fire plan, taking prisoner two companies of German infantry. Firing continued until late evening. We stayed in this position overnight, with desultory firing throughout the night.

At 0945 hrs on 1 October, a reconnaissance party left to investigate alternative gun positions, but the guns stayed where they were, firing continuously until 1715 hrs, at a rate of 29 rpg. Again we stayed here overnight, with the usual occasional bursts of firing and, at 1430 hrs on the 2nd, a new gun position was plotted, but we didn't move until 1715 hrs the following day, when we fired 25 rpg on four targets.

Still in position on the 4th, the enormous tension felt by all of us, with little respite from moving and firing, with few opportunities for relaxation and for getting a proper meal, was relieved by baths becoming available. Not in situ, of course, but probably in Helmond, where we were permitted to send a few men at a time for forty-eight hours leave. At the guns, at 1615 hrs, there came the threat from an enemy counter-attack forming up (769325) which we tried to disperse with the whole regiment firing on them. Shortly afterwards, however, at 1755 hrs, the counter-attack expanded, with enemy tanks nearby. The whole regiment of twenty-four guns was needed to repel it. Firing continued over to the next day, when further counter-attacks were mounted against us, but we managed to beat them off.

We spent an uncomfortable night in this position, maintaining a full sentry alert, which kept everyone away from sleep, tired out as they were. There was no let-up in the morning as, from 0226 hrs to 1000 hrs we shot continuously and heavily. In association with the HQ Battery Sergeant Major, I spent all this time trying frantically to maintain ammunition stocks as it was being fired as fast as we could provide it.

Then I heard that something was afoot because, having spent another restless night, the 7th was a day of coming and going. At 0730 hrs a reconnaissance party went out to survey in another gun position in the area of 717470, and 500 rounds per gun were dumped, awaiting our occupation. Even so, on the 7th we had to silence enemy mortars in support of the 3rd Monmouth Regiment, and some attention was given to the River Maas at

Vortum. The 8th saw no respite, firing all through the day, where one target was an anti-tank concentration.

These past few days had been times of great intensity and danger, and I did wonder if some of the men could go on like that indefinitely. I need not have worried, however, because not a single man grumbled and no one fell out. The 9th and 10th were simply a continuation of the previous days, until 1530 hrs when we moved off and took up a new position, both troops firing on a zero line of 120 degrees.

As noted in *Taurus Pursuant*,[6] the ensuing events appeared to everybody concerned to be complex and confusing, and therefore difficult to describe. I find myself in sympathy with this observation, but will make some attempt to unravel a patchwork situation.

The 6th was a good day for me because it was my turn to spend forty-eight hours in Helmond – my first time off duty since May, six months earlier. Together with others, I was driven to Helmond in high spirits, arriving in the evening. The gunners were billeted in an engineering factory, bedding down between the idle machines, whilst I reported to the Sergeants' Mess. First and foremost was the need for a hot bath, in which I wallowed luxuriously in the hot soapy water. A change of battledress was also available, so that by ten o'clock in the evening I was bathed, shaved and looking reasonably smart in my new rig. Then there was the supreme joy of sleeping in a real bed with clean white sheets. At 1030 hrs the next morning in the local theatre, 'Stars in Battle Dress', a show led by Charlie Chester, was put on that had us rolling in the aisles. Lunch in the Mess, with about thirty of us, was a jolly affair because we were all in the same boat, as it were, each with a few hours out of reach of a tiresome enemy. We all came from different regiments and the main concern was to let it be known that one's own regiment was far superior to any other, and that without us the war might go on forever!

The afternoon was spent sightseeing and shopping, and in the evening I returned to the theatre to see *The Chocolate Soldier* by George Bernard Shaw, acted by Richard Green and his wife Patricia Medina. On return to the Mess after the performance, there was a certain amount of 'letting one's hair down', since the Mess had acquired a substantial cellar conveniently left by the Germans. The next day was one of self-coddling as an antidote to the harsh and dangerous conditions one had just left, and to which one was about to return. In the evening, I went again to the

---

6 'A History of the 11th Armoured Division', published privately by E.R. Palamountain, 1945.

theatre and was treated to a superb performance by the Dutch Swing College Band, which would have made Glen Miller sit up and take note. All good things come to an end, however, and on the morning of 9 October I returned to the guns in the Oploo sector.

Things had not changed during my absence. Shooting had been more or less continuous, particularly on the 8th when a concentration of enemy tanks was partly destroyed, with the remainder withdrawing somewhat hastily. Targets were plentiful, and the FOOs had a field day on both the 8th and 9th.

On the 10th, amidst some desultory firing, a certain amount of reorganization took place with the arrival of replacement officers. None came our way, however, and I still retained my appointments as Acting Troop Leader, Relief GPO and sometime FOO. As I wrote earlier, I volunteered to take command of the guns at night rather than by day for reasons I never really understood, but I preferred to be awake during the night hours rather than be caught lying down.

There was always plenty to do at night to occupy oneself, in addition to firing the guns. The changeover from night duty to day duty was never clear cut, because we were constantly shooting both day and night. I could, therefore, be on the go for much of the twenty-four hours so as to be available for any contingency. One cannot curl up comfortably in a sleeping bag with the enemy on the doorstep, with four guns banging away a few yards off, always with the expectation of a sudden move. I therefore catnapped whenever it was appropriate to do so.

In the afternoon of the 10th, on a gloomy day, with darkness descending quickly, we moved again to a new position at 1530 hrs, with immediate calls for fire on a zero line of 120 degrees, and from 1620 hrs this engaged us for most of the evening. The 11th and 12th were even more exciting (if that is the right word) for around midday our Battery Commander shot the whole regiment of twenty-four guns in a massive shoot that lasted for seven minutes. Again, I was unaware of what we were firing at. This was repeated at 1345 hrs and twice again at 1700 and 1845 hrs. It was even noisier on the 12th as we engaged in an enormous fire plan, firing 300 rpg over a period of 170 minutes (two rounds per gun per minute for nearly three hours). This time we knew we were firing at a troublesome battery of *Nebelwerfers*. Later in the day we moved again to the south-east of Oploo in the direction of, and near to, Overloon, and there we had more casualties. We stayed there overnight into the 13th in some discomfort.

The weather was appalling, the drenching rain was intense and the days were permanently dark. It was bitterly cold. The locality was wooded and gloomy, the enemy were around us in some considerable numbers and the area was extensively mined. South of Oploo was not a comfortable position to be in, but there was no alternative. The first tragedy struck at 1355 hrs when, in 'C' Troop, a gun suffered a muzzle burst, where the shell, on firing, bursts prematurely at the muzzle. Sergeant Walters, who in civilian life was studying for Holy Orders, received a bad head wound, and Lance Bombardier Armistead was also wounded. At 1640 hrs we fired on a group of fifteen enemy infantrymen (728303), but at 1741 hrs the Germans mortared us in return. We silenced one of them. Firing continued through the night into the 14th.

The day was enlightened, however, when we learned that a leave party could go to Brussels for forty-eight hours and I had the agony of having to choose the first six men to go. There was no guarantee that such opportunities would continue. Sure enough, this slightly euphoric affair was soon to be shattered.

At about six o'clock in the evening, the sky was dark and lowering, with a faint moon shining through here and there. The guns were silent and we went about our respective tasks in a sombre mood. The brisk wind disturbed the coniferous trees, casting shadows that one could easily mistake for some intrepid Germans about to attack us. Our Forward Observation tank (referred to as RDon) was sited up front on the far edge of a wood that stretched out in front of us, and the crew needed supplies of fuel and food.

It fell to me to fulfil this task by going up in my Bren carrier with the necessary provisions. Driver Smith was on hand as usual and Lance Bombardier Muscoe came along too in case his mechanical skills were needed (the real reason was that not only was he a close friend of Smith, but also RDon's crew were his companions, with whom he hadn't made contact for some time). The crew of RDon warned me in some way or other that the track over which we had to go was heavily mined, as were the surrounds, but if we kept to the right side of the track, we should be safe. They only knew that because they'd gone up there themselves and got away with it. They also advised us not to break cover as the Germans were only 400 yards away to their front – which was why RDon occupied this exposed position, keeping an eye on things.

I did as I was told, with Driver Smith easing his way slowly in the dark night in first gear, through the wood along this narrow track, past a lone, empty cottage on the left that was probably the forester's accommodation in normal times, and stopping just short of the edge of the wood where RDon was hidden in the trees and well camouflaged. We managed a pleasant hour yarning about various incidents and drinking a mug of hot sweet tea, but still very conscious of the proximity of the enemy. We were a little apprehensive, too, as we had to manoeuvre our way back in the dark through the minefield. We managed it by being extra careful, sometimes stopping for me to have a closer look by getting out and examining the ground in front (it was possible to walk over some German mines because the human body did not have sufficient weight to set them off – a tank or a Bren carrier was a different matter). We eventually got back to the guns, safe and sound, thankful that it was not our job to spend the spooky night up there, although our gun position was not exactly a safe haven.

I had only been back at the guns about an hour when an order came for the journey to be repeated, the reasons for which I forget. I was engaged in some task or other at the Command Post and a newcomer, Second Lieutenant Patrick Delaforce, a very young officer, was ordered to undertake the task.

He took my Bren carrier, with Driver Smith at the wheel, and I briefed Patrick on the route to go so as to avoid the mines. He had been given different orders, however, that required a change from the route I had taken. Naturally those orders took precedence over what I had to say and I was pleased that Driver Smith was going, as he was conversant with some of the risks. Unfortunately, the changed route apparently had not been reconnoitred and the inevitable happened – the carrier was blown up on a mine. Driver Smith was killed instantly, his left leg torn off at the thigh. Patrick was injured, sustaining a severe head wound (he told me years later that he still has a piece of metal in his head).

RDon's crew at the sharp end heard the explosion and, fearing the worst, conveyed this sad news to us over the wireless. Lance Bombardier Muscoe and I immediately ran about half a mile along the track, oblivious of the mines, to the scene of the tragedy. The carrier was laid on its side, with Driver Smith's torn leg still on the clutch pedal, his body some yards away, having been pulled clear by RDon's crew. He lay lifeless under a blanket. We looked around in the dark night, out of sight of the Germans nearby, who must also have heard the explosion, amidst the proliferation of mines, for some suitable place to bury him. We were near to the forester's empty cottage and the only place we could dig a shallow grave without undue disturbance from the enemy was, incongruously, by the front door of the cottage, just where a doormat might have been placed. We buried Driver Smith, said a few words over him and forlornly made our way back. Patrick, I think, was attended to by RDon's crew.

Back at the guns, everyone anxiously wanted to know what had happened and there was great sorrow as Driver Smith was a popular member of the Troop. He was also one of the two oldest among us, having a wife and a young daughter at home. I had now lost two members of my four-man crew (Gunners Baun and Smith), together with a Bren carrier and most of my kit. What did bring a lump to my throat was to see Lance Bombardier Muscoe, sitting alone, fashioning a rough cross from some branches and, without a word to anyone, setting off on foot to place it on Smith's shallow grave. It was ironic that this day was also the first on which leave parties could go to Brussels, and Smith might have been one of them.

We could do no more, as at 0600 hrs the next day, 15 October, I moved the guns to a new position, where we were called upon to fire almost immediately on a zero line of 140 degrees. At the same time, 300 rounds per gun were delivered to the gun position, which we fired at 1030 hrs to support an attack on Overloon by 3rd British Infantry Division. Later in the day, at 1610 hrs, we fired red smoke shells on to a target to guide in the rocket-firing Typhoons flying above us in what was called a 'cab rank'.

At 0700 hrs on the 16th, the battle intensified as the Germans put in a determined counter-attack, and we had to engage them with concentrated fire, followed by a barrage. At 1200 hrs, at yet another gun position (679280), we were shooting due east at 90 degrees in support of an attack by 7th US Armoured Division to force a crossing over the Deurne Canal. At 1235 hrs we moved a little closer to the enemy at a new position (710367), where we fired 150 rounds per gun. The canal was successfully bridged at 0915 hrs on the 16th and we crossed over it in the direction of Meerselo in conformity with the Americans.

At 1600 hrs on the 17th, we engaged a battery of *Nebelwerfers* at three locations, to the extent that, by 2215 hrs, we ran dangerously short of ammunition. As it was my job to keep the guns supplied, I had a trying time getting ammunition up as we could only be approached over a very muddy track, which posed great difficulties for the wheeled trucks carrying heavy loads of 25-pdr shells (each box of four weighed a hundredweight). The weather was bad and the countryside was in an appalling state. It was an anxious and miserable time, but somehow we kept the guns firing almost non-stop.

On the 18th I led the guns to a position (734243) where we joined up with other artillery regiments firing in a counter-battery role controlled by a single FOO. We stayed in that position until 1450 hrs on the 19th when we moved off to Weaverloo. The Germans were putting up a determined resistance literally yard by yard and we were continuously in action throughout the 19th, 20th and 21st, staying at the latter position which we occupied at 1758 hrs, remaining there until the 22nd (further parties from the guns were able to take their forty-eight hours rest in Helmond).

The 22nd saw us in a position at Meerselo (731258) and we stayed there for two more days, but then had a busy time firing 87 rounds per gun at who knows what? The 26th proved to be a little more exciting because we were stumbled upon by a German patrol, but were able to see them off. The 27th was also tense when we came in to support the 3rd Monmouths who were booby-trapping a building. Later, at 1715 hrs, we fired 50 rounds per gun in support of a deliberate infantry advance.

This slow type of fighting was not entirely to our liking – we were trained to be highly mobile in the best cavalry tradition, but this was a process of grim attrition, although we did make some progress at the same time. We had become, in fact, field artillery, which fulfilled a different role to which we were largely unaccustomed. However, the next three days occupied us quite well. On the 29th, for instance, the Germans were successful in an attack through Meigel and Leisel, as a result of which all guns and tanks were alerted to the possibility of close attacks on them. On the 30th, we were able to do some much-needed calibration of the guns, using the camera method, but at1715 hrs we had to fire another 87 rounds per gun on assorted targets to repel any further enemy action in our direction. Similarly, the next day we fired another 67 rounds per gun (some 4 tons per Troop of high explosive) to complete this local operation.

By now the gunners had almost become automatons. We rarely knew at the time what we were shooting at, and it was just a matter of carrying out the drill of loading and firing the guns. We knew that what we were doing was of crucial importance and I knew that my four gun sergeants, who I firmly believed to be the best in the Regiment, were experts in their job, and they gave their all. I tried, therefore, when I was in charge at the Troop Command Post, to describe targets and for this information to be passed on to the guns.

The month of November continued with its daily hate of rain, sleet, snow and freezing temperatures. The absence of all creature comforts and of having to work in permanently wet clothing might, in other circumstances, have taken its toll, but surprisingly not a man in my Troop ever reported sick – not even when one of the exhausted gunners drank almost a pint of Calvados in the middle of the night in mistake for water!

As in the First World War, the Germans were sticklers for routine and there were predictable times when we knew they would be hostilely active. The enemy attacks on the 30th and 31st were almost identical – they even repeated the same routine on 1 November, at precisely the same, 1715 hrs, when we fired back at them at a rate of 48 rounds per gun. And, just to show they meant it, the Germans did it again on the 2nd, again at the same time, causing us to expend a further 30 rounds per gun in retaliation. The next two days were moderately quiet, but the weather was appalling. The 5th was a good day for us as it saw the return to the Troop of our respected Troop Commander, Captain Phillip Kinnersley. Having been wounded on Hill 112 during Operation Epsom, he was now back in action with us.

Our role in the next few days was not extensive. The current strategy was to clear the Maas pocket of all enemy troops, which was not going to be easy. The scarcity of roads, their appalling condition and the swampy nature of the Peel countryside largely precluded the use of tanks, including us. This was the task of 159 Infantry Brigade, under whose command we must have come because we took part in scuffles at a small railway station, oddly named America and Meteoric. I recall us pausing in the yard of the little railway station, after we captured it, and discovering an abandoned omnibus. I entertained the thought that it might make a good Troop Command Post but despite Lance Bombardier Muscoe's mechanical skills, we couldn't get the engine to work.

On the 6th, however, we were formally pulled out of the line, for at 1000 hrs the Troop moved to De Rips for rest and maintenance, with some fortunate men spending twenty-four hours leave in Antwerp. We stayed in De Rips until the 10th, then moved back to the previous gun position, but 1230 hrs saw us in action again as we fired a few rounds. For the first time there was a real anxiety about the supply of ammunition. The port of Antwerp was not in full operation and supplies still had to come over the long haul from way back. We were therefore limited to expending no more that 29 rounds per gun per day, although quite how that peculiar figure was calculated was not known to us lesser mortals.

On 14 November, some reorganization at troop level took place. Captain Kinnersley took command of the Troop (on the 15th he was awarded the Military Cross) and Lieutenant John Alford became the GPO. Charles Coad, who had done the job of GPO so well in the most trying of circumstances, therefore became Troop Leader, leaving me to revert solely to the job of Battery Sergeant Major. Even so, I only lasted one day in that position, as Charles was drafted to being a FOO and I became the Acting Troop Leader again. At the same time Sergeant Musker, whose Sexton had broken down on the Belgian frontier at Pecq ten weeks earlier, rejoined us, complete with his crew, but minus the Sexton.

Matters then became somewhat confusing as on 17th our Battery Commander found himself directing the fire of eight Sherman tanks, while over the next two days all our observation posts had to be handed over to 30th Field Regiment, Royal Artillery. We were directed, along with 3 RTR, to Deurne. The next day, the 20th, we took over the gun positions of our sister regiment, 151st Ayrshire Yeomanry, RA. It seems that there were three operations going on at the time, called Brigand, Barbican and Nutcracker, and we were called upon to fire in support of Brigand at about 0700 hrs on the 22nd, moving off at 1345 hrs to another position (736226).

Early the following morning, at 0625 hrs, the Germans came into action with their 88mm guns and about fifteen shells landed amongst us. Don Troop was sited immediately to the rear of Charlie Troop and the shells fell mostly between us. Fortunately there were no casualties, although there was some damage to the equipment. We stayed in this position for three miserable days. The rain and sleet seemed to be unceasing, and it was bitterly cold. There was some small respite to come, however, for at 0715hrs on the 26th we moved away (636331) out of the immediate action zone, and enjoyed some rest and maintenance. We had three good days catching up with things that had been neglected for far too long, but on the 29th, at 0830 hrs, we moved to Horst and took on a number of targets in Venlo. Firing continued over the next few hours and into the next day, culminating on 30 November in a concentrated fire plan called Swansea.

On 1 December, the tanks of 29th Armoured Brigade were withdrawn from active operations and moved to the area of Ypres and Ostend, to enable their Sherman tanks to be replaced by the newer and better-armoured Comet tanks. These new tanks were armed with a 17-pdr gun, capable of narrowing the discrepancy in firepower between the heavier German tanks and ours. However, we were not part of this changeover and it was our lot to remain in action. This welcome changeover in tanks was interrupted by the great German offensive launched from the Ardennes on 16 December, and 3 RTR, for instance, had to give up their new Comet tanks on which they were being retrained, and go back to their old Shermans as they were called upon to operate alongside the Americans when the Germans made some headway.

In the early days of December, we learned that 11th Armoured Division was to have a change of sector, extending from Maeseyck to Roermond, but for the moment we were fully engaged in beating off limited German attacks. On the 5th, we took over positions formerly held by the Ayrshire Yeomanry and found ourselves at a place called Brockhuizen (909221), close to the west bank of the River Maas, staying there until 1000 hrs on the 9th, when we were ordered elsewhere (871189).

There was no let-up in the bad weather. The incessant rain and sleet had been intense, and the flat countryside was waterlogged in many places. It continued to be very cold, with low cloud cover and fog. On the 17th our rate of firing had slowed down, but not so with the Germans. That day the enemy mortared Charlie Troop nearby and although it was extremely unpleasant, they had no casualties. Fortunately, we moved out of this nasty position and the next day the Troop moved back to Brockhuixen in heavy snow.

It was in this inhospitable area that, at 1200 hrs on the 21st, we occupied an action position near Kinroy (9084). For a short time the weather cleared (in relative terms). The rain stopped and a wintry sun shone on the ice-covered ground. It was now Christmas Day and we determined to observe it in the traditional manner (hoping that the Germans might do the same). There was a farm close by occupied by a surly pro-German farmer, from whom we demanded tables – he could hardly have refused. We set them up on the frozen ground and laid out the rations sent up to us. There was plenty of tinned turkey, tinned potatoes and vegetables, and even tinned Christmas pudding, all washed down by an assortment of alcoholic beverages. We were dressed in a variety of garments, scarves, balaclavas and mittens in an effort to keep warm, but it did not prevent us from tucking in. In true British Army tradition, the officers and sergeants served up the food and waited upon the men. The farmer was not amused. On the 29th we were on the move again, this time to Ophoven and Maesecyck. Unusually, we were more or less free from enemy action as their attention was elsewhere in the Ardennes battle.

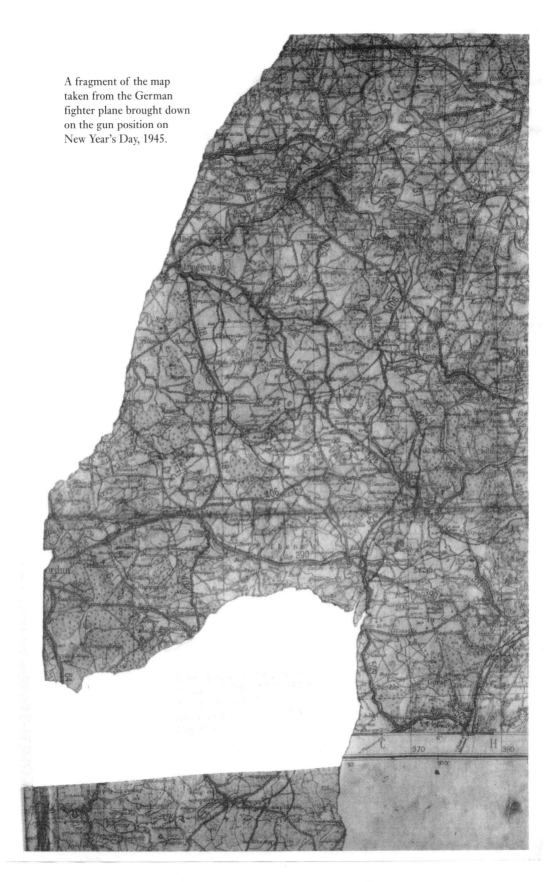

A fragment of the map
taken from the German
fighter plane brought down
on the gun position on
New Year's Day, 1945.

New Year's Day was quite eventful, however. It was the day that Hitler ordered an all-out assault by the Luftwaffe on Allied airfields and hundreds of enemy planes took to the air. Don Troop occupied a position where the ground rose gently to a small plateau. Charlie Troop, 200 yards in front of us, occupied the upper, flattish ground. We watched the German planes going over (and some coming down); the Bofors anti-aircraft section attached to us was having a field day.

I had some reason to visit my opposite number, BSM Sidney Beresford, in Charlie Troop, and began walking up towards his position. Halfway, there was a lot of banging going on and, looking up, I saw a German fighter plane, with what seemed to be guns blazing, flying at ground level directly towards me. There was no cover and I simply clawed the ground.

To my amazement and relief the plane crashed to the ground about a hundred yards in front of me. What I had thought were wing guns firing, were not – the plane was on fire, having been shot down by the Bofors gunners. However, one of the undercarriage wheels became detached in the crash and bounced at speed straight towards me. Still lying prone, all I could do was to roll sideways, which was just as well as it sped by within a yard or so. It was a very close shave, indeed.

This incident did not end there. When I recovered my senses and looked around, I saw a hand a short distance away – just a hand, no body! I carefully examined it, without touching it. It was a small hand, torn off at the wrist, and was one clearly not used to hard labour. It was no bigger than a girl's hand and looked very much like one. It had belonged to the unfortunate pilot of the crashed plane and I realized that he must have been very young (we learned later that eighteen year olds were recruited as pilots, with only a few hours training). I buried the hand in situ.

I also retrieved the map the pilot may have used for navigation (see page 145). It was a small-scale map covering a vast area and I still wonder what use to him it might have been.

This period, in the early days of January 1945, was mostly one of 'standing to'. The two main efforts were directed at stopping the Germans' advance beyond Bastogne in their attempt to reach Antwerp, and so bring about a split between the American and Allied Forces. We were not involved in either of these operations.

Around this time we took up a position at Roggel, formerly occupied by a Field Artillery Regiment of the 51st Highland Division. The extremely bad weather returned and deep snow lay frozen on the ground. Our relative inaction meant that we could man the guns with skeleton crews, leaving the others to forage around in search of creature comforts. Troop headquarters' staff occupied a two-storey barn, using the upper floor for rest and relaxation. Even so, the Germans did not leave us entirely alone, shelling the immediate area intermittently, seemingly in random fashion. Some shells came unpleasantly close.

I, too, took advantage of this relative inaction and made myself comfortable with the aid of straw and hay. I was reading a book and came to a part that had me laughing my head off. This happened to coincide with a shell exploding nearby, and the combination of both book and bang caused the assembled company to believe that at long last I had gone off my rocker! What actually was happening was that I was reading *Three Men in a Boat*, and had reached the point where Harris tries to open a tin of something without the aid of a tin opener, watched by Montmorency the bemused dog. I found it intensely amusing, which for the moment drove out any thoughts of the danger we were in. The men thought differently.[7]

On or about 13 or 14 January, in bitterly cold weather, with daylight fading as early as 1500 hrs, the Troop Commander, Captain Kinnersley, asked me to accompany him to a forward observation post, which was sited in an empty villa on the west bank of the River Maas near to Brockhuizen. The villa was built almost at the river's edge and the river itself was probably 150 or 200 yards wide, and fast flowing. On the opposite side, directly in our view, a lane led down to the river at right angles to the bank, with a cottage on each side facing one another. The Germans, who were doing exactly the same job as us, occupied these. We just stared at each other.

It was very spooky. We were entirely alone, clearly in view of the enemy. Just to emphasize the confused situation, we knew that during the hours of darkness the Germans sent a patrol across the river and probably occupied our house. Every morning, therefore, we mounted the stairs leading to the upper floors with great trepidation, armed only with revolvers, not knowing whether an enemy patrol was still there, or even if they had booby-trapped it. On occupying the room that looked out over the river, we had to sit motionless for hours, from eight in the morning to about three in the afternoon. We sat on rickety chairs, peering across the river from

---

7 Two or three years ago, I attended a theatre where Rodney Bews (*The Likely Lads*) was giving a one-man performance of an adaptation of *Three Men in a Boat*, and at the end of the show I met him in the bar and told him this story. It earned me a beer!

behind a ragged lace curtain. It was bitterly cold, made worse by bodily inaction, as we dare not move in case the Germans spotted us. If they did, they were likely to train their machine guns in our direction. They were already firing on fixed lines all around us. For some reason, we had strict orders that if they did intensify their activities, we were not to retaliate.

On leaving this inhospitable villa each day as darkness fell, we had to make our way cautiously to the rear, avoiding as best we could the enemy's tracer bullets that sprayed the area. Our destination was some form of institutional building currently occupied by an infantry battalion, possibly the Durham Light Infantry, who were guarding this section of the Maas. We spent uncomfortable nights there, one of which was livened by being offered a bowl of daffodil soup – the so-called cook thought the bulbs he had found in the cellars were onions.

A day or so later, at close to 1500 hrs, a message was received that required me to report immediately to the Battery Commander. This meant that I had to crawl in the dark on my hands and knees for a quarter of a mile, over frozen ground, to avoid being hit by the enemy machine gun that never seemed to stop firing. Fortunately it was using tracer so one could time one's movements as the machine gun weaved around.

I reached the Battery Commander's billet safely, not knowing what to expect. He was waiting for me and offered me a large glass of whisky, which was most welcome.[8] He then informed me that I was to return to England the next day. I thought at first I was being sacked, but it seemed that I was to go on a Long Gunnery Staff Course at the School of Artillery. I protested but he said the war was nearly over and that as a regular soldier I had my future career to think about. He thanked me for my efforts over the past eight months, and so that, for me, was the end of my war in the face of the enemy.

Later, in England, I learned that, on his recommendation, I had been awarded the Military Cross, which at that time was a rare honour for a Warrant Officer Class II.

---

8 Over fifty years later I met Major Smythe-Osborne at a HAC reunion dinner, where he again offered me a large whisky. Sadly, he had lost an arm some weeks after we parted in 1945.

# *Appendix I*

# Author's Citation for the
# Military Cross

—ᴍ—

*London Gazette*, 29 March 1945

The Military Cross

No. 849722 Warrant Officer Class II (Battery Sergeant Major) Ernest Arthur Powdrill, Royal Horse Artillery (East Kirby, Nottinghamshire).

'BSM Powdrill is the Troop Sergeant Major of "D" Troop of a battery of RHA, HAC. He has been a tower of strength to his Troop throughout the advance from Beny Bocage to Holland. His complete indifference to personal danger, his cheerfulness and resourcefulness have been a fine example to his Troop. He has done the job of Troop Leader continuously and Relief Gun Position Officer when officers have been casualties.

At Le Desert in August, the Regiment was threatened by German infantry who infiltrated on all sides – they were supported by Panthers. BSM Powdrill went out as Forward Observation Officer, dispersed a small band of German infantry, located the Panthers and remained in observation until forced to withdraw by heavy Spandau fire from his rear. By his prompt resourcefulness on this occasion, he prevented what had every appearance of developing into a most troublesome situation.

During the long advance, he was frequently left many miles behind with Sextons which were damaged, but never failed to locate his unit and bring up the stragglers safely, although the country was full of German infantry who had not been mopped up. At times, when the gun positions were being heavily shelled, he was always at hand to deal with the wounded, and took immediate charge of any difficult situation.'

# *Index*